Teenagers, Wake Up!

The Awakening Call from a Teen to a Teen

Samantha de Senna Fernandes

To my parents and sister,

for unconditionally loving and supporting me

through thick and thin.

And to God,

for giving me abundant wisdom.

CONTENTS

CHAPTER ONE: WHY WAKE UP?

I am Samantha de Senna Fernandes, and I am 16 years old. I was diagnosed with a rare skin condition called *Incontinentia Pigmenti* ("IP" for short) when I was only four days old. IP symptoms can include hair loss, dental abnormalities, intellectual disabilities, and serious blindness. Fun fact: if I were an XY-chromosome bearer, I likely wouldn't have made it after those four days.

Apart from hyperpigmentation on my skin, I have no other symptoms, and I'm blessed to remain in the best health condition possible for my age, even after my various near-death experiences. The best part is that the pigments fade over time, and they will have totally disappeared by the time I make it into my twenties, which isn't the case for others like me. This aspect of my life still plays a huge role in why I am who I am today. It is one of the many things I will forever be grateful for.

Even though I was lucky this way, many people intentionally made me feel unaccepted for something I couldn't change about myself, even if I wanted to. This resulted in me becoming more sensitive than others. Unlike most people my age, I spent much of my time reflecting on life's different aspects, which helped deepen my understanding of the gift of life.

There was one point where I looked around and realized that teenagers from my generation lack their own specialty. They lack a voice. Some don't even know their potential or how to use it to shine in their own unique way. Many can't even fight for their worth. The saddest part is, the majority of today's teens aren't willing to do productive things to benefit themselves, or independently make wise decisions. With that in mind, I got fed up. And this is where it all began.

During the darkest time of my life, when I had just turned fourteen, the idea of writing my insights down sparked off, amidst everything. And that spark is this book.

In addition to this, I have set up an online platform at www.richmindz.com, where teens have the chance to talk to me one-on-one, about any difficulty they are facing in relation to the topics I cover in this book. You can find my blogs there as well. I have also started my very own *The RichMindz Podcast*, which is available on any downloading and streaming platform. Teens of many ages gather there to share their thoughts and insights on current youth social issues we face as a generation.

Even though I myself didn't receive much help from my peers during rough seas, I started all of this in hopes of inspiring other teens to open their eyes and do the great things they are capable of doing. Most of us are sleeping through our adolescent years, wasting our precious time in meaningless activities when we could be truly growing, becoming strong and independent people, and preparing ourselves for a life of real greatness and true happiness. That's why we need to wake up now to all that we are missing. Pulling back the curtain and showing you what that is, is the purpose of this book.

You may not always like what you read here. Most of the time, hopefully, you will. I think these ideas strike the bell of truth more often than not. And when they do, it means they resonate with you. I only ask that you read with an open mind and be willing to consider a different perspective.

Now, with all of my strength, I am here to call out to my fellow teenagers...

WAKE UP!

Chapter Two: Your Two Most Undervalued Treasures

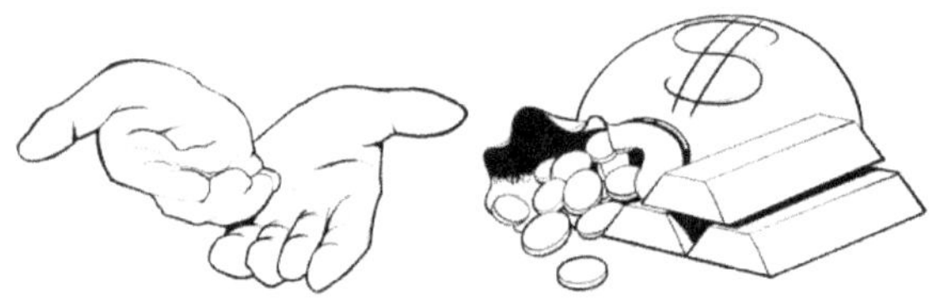

"Today be thankful and think how rich you are. Your family is priceless, your time is gold, and your health is wealth."

~ Zig Ziglar

For others it may differ, but for me, both family and health have always come first. They are the two main things one cannot survive without—the biggest blessings that conquer *all*. However, not a lot of people see that. And because of this, the two have grown to become very underrated, even when they deserve recognition and awareness.

Even when hardships came into play, my family never gave up on me. When I was extremely sick, my parents took time off work just to be with me 24/7, always ensuring my happiness and safety. They raised and cherished me just like any other parent would with their child, despite my condition, and how I cherish them in return.

But what if they gave up on me? What if my pigments were to never fade? What if I grew blind? What if my *life* was cut short? I could have died at least ten times, but here I am, still standing, alive and well after everything. This still fascinates me, even though it happened years ago. This is why, amidst all the chaos, I was called "the miracle child."

But there were times when I would imagine the life I was supposed to live—one that would have been hard to cope with. If you haven't experienced the extremities of health, you have no idea how blessed you are to be born with no complications and without any disease occurring in your body.

Think about it. You could possess everything you've ever dreamt of—all the riches, diamonds, gold, top-branded clothing, huge mansions, and private jets. You could be the world's richest person, but without health, your life would be difficult to cope with. As the saying goes, "Money can't buy you happiness." It can, but that sort of happiness is short-term. Both family and health are things that will remain with you wherever you go. They are the main and permanent sources of true love and real happiness, not materialistic designer handbags or shoes that are stowed or thrown away after being worn several times.

Picture your life now without your family and your health. You would be set back from everything, and your world would be turned upside down. If you have both family and health, it's time you start acknowledging how blessed you are, because once they are gone, you practically lose everything.

"Families are like branches on a tree.
We grow in different directions, yet our
roots remain as one."

The Influences of Family

Over the years, I started to have this habit of studying people during my free time (which sounds a tad creepy, but I promise you, it isn't what it seems). What I mean is, I would observe people and try to understand why they came to be a certain way, why they had certain language, habits, and intentions toward other people— just their behavior in general. By doing this, you can anticipate the kind of life the person is set to have, and especially the kind of family they were (or are being) brought up in.

Let's take a bully as an example. Maybe this person is brought up in a family that spoils them, which makes them too proud, leading them to take that energy of entitlement to school every day. Or they may be the least prioritized sibling in a family that doesn't give them enough love and attention.

Whichever family bullies may belong to, they feel the need to get all the attention and praise at school just to feel important during the day. Then later in the evening, they go home either still as a VIP, or they return to being a "nobody." Now, this is what it's like to "read" someone like a book.

This is how family plays a huge role in who we grow to be as individuals. People will always learn from the behavior they are surrounded by. This is why you need to honestly contemplate whether your family members are good influences in your life.

If your family somehow fails to be a good influence, this doesn't give you an excuse to follow in their footsteps and end up being just like them. You are independent enough to know what is best for yourself. Also be aware of the way your parents speak to you, because that will probably be your inner voice throughout your entire life.

For example, if your parents are extremely strict and put a lot of pressure on you, then it's likely you will be strict with yourself and put a lot of pressure on yourself, which can damage your mental health a lot. Don't let what others say to you turn into the voice inside your own head. It's your own responsibility to make sure you remain unaffected by something like that. This is something you need to be observant about in friendships and relationships, too.

In relationships, get to know your partner's family well, even if you are head over heels for them. Pay attention to whether their family is welcoming and whether they have good relationships with each other. Observe the way your partner treats both of your families, because this will determine how they will treat the family you might have with them in the future.

The way they treat other people, such as waiters in a restaurant, also shows their true colors. This helps you think before getting into a committed relationship with someone. In friendships, note that your friends mostly reflect their parents. So if their parents are known to not be great people, there is a possibility that they might turn out just like them, or even worse.

Speaking about friends, sometimes my own would ask me for advice on personal issues. We talk for a while, everything is fine until I mention the word 'parents'. Once I ask, "Have you spoken about this with your parents?" or "What do your parents think?" the friend freaks out and says, "Oh, no, my parents and I have never been that close," or "I find it weird opening up to them," or "They never listen to me anyway, so what's the point?"

The point is, this is a serious problem. Teens nowadays hardly ask their parents for help because of these exact reasons. They have grown up to become damaged because they never saw their parents' usefulness in helping them with life problems. But isn't that the reason *why* parents exist? If they don't listen and look out for you, what purpose do they serve that entitles them to still be called a parent? Being a parent is a role, not some label with no meaning to it. Parents exist to shed light on you at all times, mainly during your darkest hours. They exist to guide you through transitions and tough phases and to redirect your path when you go astray.

In times of struggle, I sought help from friends, too. I came to realize one thing: their advice was all similar. That's because they all shared the same viewpoint, the same mentality. Some of my friends weren't even able to suggest any solutions. However, when I shared my problems with my parents, their approach was completely different. I didn't only learn interesting things from their experiences and perspectives, but I also learned how not to repeat the same mistakes they made decades ago. And how did I do that? I just listened attentively to what they had to say and absorbed it. You might be thinking, "That sounds too easy," or "I always listen to my parents, but I still end up doing stupid things." Well, here's the thing. You probably aren't really listening.

We ask for life advice from our parents, but once we hear them say, "When I look back...," we switch off from hearing what comes next. We immediately assume that we're going to hear stories we've already heard before.

The stories that we could memorize off by heart if we wanted to—stories that don't apply to us whatsoever. Or we think we can do better than them anyway, and because of this ignorance and pride that we hold, we lose interest. We just nod, stare into space, and don't even bother hearing what they have to say. We all do this, and we all know the drill!

But coming to think of it, it's really unfortunate. Our parents may be trying to tell us, "Don't make the same mistake I made," or "I was foolish back then." That's probably the most important information they could ever give as a reflection and judgment on their own experiences, as it's what they have learned after everything. So make sure your eyes are fully open, along with your ears, when you talk with your parents.

Doing this will even save you time from fixing or getting involved in problems that you could have easily avoided if you had just listened. If you don't seek their seasoned advice, you will find yourself making the same mistakes your parents made decades ago, and it will happen to you repeatedly until you eventually *learn*—which will be a long road you will have no choice but to take. This is one of the many side effects of not paying attention to your parents' words of wisdom.

This especially applies to you if you are going through bullying or other sorts of serious issues. I'll be sharing more about this later on, but if serious things are happening to you, you must tell your parents. You mustn't completely rely on your friends, because they won't know what to do or how to help you, apart from listening to your cries.

In situations like these, your parents are always a better solution because they have more authority than you and your friends put together. After all, it's what family is for. And never fear speaking to them, because things will be dealt with immediately once you involve an adult. The more you hide the problem, the more you are putting off the situation from being fixed.

Scared of Opening Up?

Are you scared of opening up to your parents? Are you worried that you will get judged? This sort of fear usually stems from a weak child-parent relationship, which results in the child never turning to their parents in times of need. Kids who grow up believing their parents are unable to love or take care of them, grow into adults who have trouble loving and taking care of themselves. This belief builds into a huge inner conflict, and a habitual way of thinking it's hard to overcome. This is exactly what starts off a strong base of insecurity and a lack of self-esteem, often leading kids to seek love and attention in not-so-great places.

To avoid this from happening, go ask your parents for advice before it's too late. Doing this will build trust between you. Your parents won't be annoyed if you approach them, and it won't be awkward, if that is what you are thinking. I bet they are just patiently waiting for you to open up, wondering when you will break free from your shell and show up at their door.

Don't be that awkward teen who hides in their room all day on the phone. Have some social time. Tell your parents about how your day went, share some recent school gossip for a laugh. Make an effort—whether it means talking about your problems or just sharing how you feel in general. Do this for your own benefit. There's no need to hide.

Even if you aren't close with them or if you don't see eye-to-eye, this is something you should work toward as of now. This also applies to siblings. Talk out your differences, but mainly why you feel this way and how it started. Being open is something everyone fears, especially when you are opening up to someone you feel distant from. On the bright side, remember that taking this step forward can at least reduce awkwardness and complications between you, big or small. But note that this process takes time. This is why it's baby steps. Practice this often, and you'll find there will be a huge difference between later on and back then.

Indulge the process. Who knows? The end result might be completely unexpected, but highly positive. They might even open up, too, and you might get to know them a lot more than before. Whether they do or not, at least you will feel more confident and accepted, both you and your problems. Feeling this slight ounce of alleviation and acceptance is a sign that you are already one step closer to developing and progressing your relationship with your family. But remember, you need to keep it going.

Knowing that you have your parents' support, you'll grow into someone capable of self-love and self-acceptance. If you haven't allowed your parents to give you their support, because you insist on there being a wall between you, this won't only affect the way you see yourself, but it may also deeply scar your relationship with your future spouse and children. The cycle will repeat further down the line, with the next generation, simply because you failed to accept and give familial love in the first place. Try and not be guilty of that dumb mistake.

It's the Little Things that Matter

Looking at the negative side, you could make the following acronym using the letters in the word "parents." Aren't they all so…

P - Petty

A - Annoying

R - Ridiculous

E - Evil

N - Nosy

T - Talkative

S - Sickening

Relatable? I think so, too. We are all tempted to stand firm with that acronym, but amidst all this, we need to consider that parents are also…

P - Powerful

A - Amazing

R - Responsible

E - Empathetic

N - Noble

T - Trustworthy

S - Special

Oftentimes, we must turn things around to realize what truly is in front of us. If we apply this to parents, yes, they can be pestering at times, but they rock as parents. Not everyone can ace that role, and some aren't blessed to have parents like yours. Plus, it can easily be forgotten that being a parent is one of the most difficult and stressful jobs in the universe.

You can never imagine just how much they truly treasure you, not until you open your eyes. I want you to celebrate the love you receive every day. Count all the blessings you've received from your parents so far, because, trust me, the more blessings you count, the more you will get in return when your time of being a parent comes—which is a very daunting stage of life.

Once you have a family of your own, you'll immediately understand the stress your parents underwent while raising you. All the little things they did behind the scenes just to make sure you were properly taken care of, and the many ways they managed everything to keep the household and all essential things up and running— all done just for you. For example, do you know how much a sofa costs? How about a bed? You see? This is exactly what I mean. It's absolutely normal not to know the price of simple things because we just have it all.

When you were only the size of a pea, you were instinctively put first by your parents, who longed to warmly welcome you into this world. And since you are now obviously greater than the size of a pea, no words could ever describe how much more they would do for you now. So the next time you sit on your cozy sofa or sleep in your warm bed, think about your parents and appreciate their effort, because one day, when you go furniture shopping for your own house, only then will you realize how expensive a sofa or a bed can be, and how much more costly a comfortable mattress is on top of that.

Parents are also constantly paying bills and settling mortgages. Just saying those two words already brings complications to the table. Not to mention that there are tons of other stressful things your parents have to deal with at the same time. Your parents are also paying for your education so that you can at least have a chance to expand your knowledge on various subjects. Even if you think your school sucks or you think the things you're currently learning are useless, at least you're still *able* to attend a school, while that only happens in the dreams of other children.

This is why you should take this opportunity to be grateful for the little, day-to-day blessings you barely notice. Thank your parents every time, even for the small things, because you wouldn't have any of it if it weren't for them. Take a minute every night to acknowledge how much effort has constantly been invested in things such as keeping you safe, ensuring your health, checking in on your feelings, taking care of all your necessities for you, making sure you have enough money to spend, planning all those memorable trips—the list is endless. But above all, providing you with food, clothing, and an actual roof to live under.

You don't even need to think about your next meal. You don't need to be anxious about having enough blankets to sleep under tonight. You don't need to worry about these things at all when other kids do, simply because your parents have already made sure that you will be provided for unconditionally.

Our Selfishness

Even if your parents have given you everything and beyond, one day you will look back and realize how badly you often treated them. The times you argued over something petty or raised your voice because you were just too arrogant to admit your mistakes. Or because you were mad at them for not getting the Wi-Fi fixed within the first few hours of it being broken. Or the minute you hated them because the other sibling got the better phone or the bigger bedroom. I myself have done a fair share of these, and I admit I am guilty of it, and deep down, you know you are, too. You did all of this back when you were younger, when you didn't truly acknowledge their feelings.

Imagine your child lashing out at you for something. Of course, they would never understand that all you did was try to do the best thing for them. And being poorly treated like this, you would stop and wonder: "How could someone I birthed and raised, someone I love *so* dearly, still end up treating me like this, even after I sacrificed everything just for them? How is this fair? What have I done to deserve this?" Yes, it sounds heart-breaking and disappointing, right? This is the sort of thing that runs through your own parents' minds. All I am saying is, I hope this isn't you right there, and it better not be.

Even when this happens when you behave badly, your parents will try to compromise and empathize with you and find ways to fix what went wrong. They will always let it slide by giving you excuses like, "It's just puberty. It's normal," or "You're just having a bad day," or "It's okay, sweetie, you don't need to apologize"—even when there shouldn't be a single excuse for treating them terribly. They give you that excuse because they will never be able to picture you as the bad guy, even if you literally are. They love you too much to do that. They have seen you at your worst, and they still think you're the best. And this is the joy of having amazing parents.

They have to manage you and your problems, and their own parents' problems too. It's irritating having two generations burying you with burdening issues, so please go easy on them and be a good kid. They don't deserve your salty attitude, let alone an inch of hate when all they do is love. Make their lives easier by taking care of yourself instead. Parents are the most precious and incredible beings on Earth. They are our heroes. Not Iron Man or the amazing Spider-Man you praise on television, but our real-world superheroes—those who deserve more recognition. Therefore, of course, we must treat them with high respect, no matter what.

So, with that being said, if your parents scold you for something you did, just contain your comebacks. Firing back with the same negative energy won't make anything better, and it won't make you any superior to them. All your words will do is just hurt people, which will create a much bigger problem than there was to begin with. Your parents aren't big fans of telling you off anyway, but they are still doing their job, teaching and educating you for your own benefit.

This is another good time to listen to them, since it's their most honest opinion on the areas you should improve in as a person. Choosing to ignore that only results in your parents telling you off for the same thing over and over again, until you finally decide to own up to your responsibility and do better. They are also doing it partly because they need to slightly let their anger out because they have had to bottle up all the emotions you might have caused them to feel.

The Person behind the Superhero Mask

Speaking of feelings, we are all so used to seeing our parents happy that we don't even notice the effort they put into making *us* crack a smile. They focus on our happiness until they eventually forget their own because they would rather see us happy, even if this means sacrificing their own happiness. Not to sound cheesy, but their happiness only exists when we are happy.

But even when their total focus is on our joy, at times they might feel like they have disappointed us, thinking they could have done so much more even when they have given their all. When you're down or when you cry, your parents can't help but guiltily blame themselves, saying that they should've prevented you from feeling this way, whether it was their own fault or not. Then they will wonder what went wrong and try to come up with solutions to make you smile again.

Sometimes parents will try so hard up to the point where they come off as weird, awkward, and embarrassing. But what we don't know is that they are like this because they're nervous, but they will still do their best to cheer you up anyway. This just proves that any battle you fight is ten times the scale for your parents, without exaggeration. They want to help and fight alongside you, whatever the battle you may face in life.

But when they fight their own battles, they try so hard to not show negative emotions in front of you, because all they want to display is how much of a pro they are when handling things, how to be strong and how to set a good example, just for you. This is why you will barely be able to spot their vulnerability. Don't forget, they are also under a lot of pressure trying to keep up with your expectations of them, which are presumably never-ending. We all expect way too much from our parents, forgetting that they are only human.

So when it's their turn being down, be the one to comfort them. Next time, ask *them* to open up to *you*. Perhaps they might not have a friend to rely on. So be their friend, as they are yours in your times of struggle and need. Remind them that they are also accepted and understood, like how they do with you all the time, regardless of whether or not you are having a bad day. This time, *you* can be the one who makes *them* feel safe.

It's your job as their child to show them you are there for them and how much you care about them in return, because in reality, you will never, ever be able to repay all those sleepless nights they spent trying to put you to sleep; the seven thousand times they had to change your diapers; the rushes to the hospital when you had a fever in the middle of the night; the times they were worried sick and stressed out about your safety and your friendships at school.

One day when your parents have grown all grey and old, it will be you putting them to sleep. It will be you changing their diapers. It will be you rushing them to the hospital. It will be you worrying whether your parents have enough friends to keep them company while you're busy at work. Think of it as a role reversal. How fascinating is life?

As parents, they will be spending almost three-quarters of their life doing one thing: worrying about you. I cannot make things any clearer than this. So try to not be a pain in the ass. Do as you are told, and I can assure you that the outcome will be great. The last thing your parents want to do is to fail you, so make the effort to not fail them. Ensure them that you will live the bright future they have always dreamt of you having. All they want to see you do in life is excel, so please try to not disappoint them.

If you do by choice, remember: guilt is always right around the corner. It's a very powerful and consuming thing, which actually drives your parents to give you the great and beyond. You need to learn how to do the same. Value them when they are here because, sooner or later, you'll regret not spending enough time with them, as they grow older by the second. And don't forget, you are growing older by the second, too.

The older you become, the more you will realize that the only reason why your parents "annoyingly controlled" you all along was because they wanted to make sure you got the best from what was there. But you still need to be able to limit how controlling they are. If they are going through your phone, social media, or reading your diary, then this is where trust for them is lost. They must respect your privacy instead of invading it and limiting you from exploring and growing.

At the same time, you must be responsible enough not to rely only on your parents to educate you. Somewhere along the journey of life, we all need to grow up, and now's as good a time as any to get started. We are teenagers, not babies who need pampering. Constantly relying on your parents to force you to drink water, do your homework, wash the dishes, and do your own laundry shows that you aren't ready for the transition to adulthood. You only have less than a decade to get used to taking care of yourself until it's time to move out on your own, so isn't it time to start moving in the direction of self-sufficiency?

And when you do move out, your life will change forever. From that moment, it will be your *own* responsibility to ensure that this change is for the better. For many kids, that change turns them into becoming too proud, too confident, and too independent. They take up the classic bad habits like smoking, drinking, or drugs. All of these are things you can easily resort to, especially since your parents aren't in control of your life anymore.

But note one thing: even though you might have thought your parents were controlling your life, they actually weren't. You were in control the whole time, and you *still* are in control. Your parents are only there to guide you until you leave the nest. Your behavior doesn't depend on their decisions. It always depends on yours. You have free will all along, and it's all a test to see how far you can go with that.

Worst-case scenario is you ending up doing stupid things by choice, and you will spend your whole life making amends for it. No matter how "strictly educated" you were at home, you can easily forget what you learned during your decades of education and discipline and go astray according to your own decisions. Your parents won't forbid you from doing those things. They will let you choose. After all, you control where you go in life. But make sure not to let your present decisions, distractions, and influences ruin your standing later on in life.

Once you are all grown up and ready to completely move out from the home you were brought up in, you will not live in that small room that was yours, in that house on that street. You will start to miss your family like never before, and you'll wish you could have done more to honor them. You will remember all of the little yet special moments you shared and all of the childhood memories that happened to you and only you, giving you uniqueness and everlasting joy. You will begin to realize that your parents actually did an amazing job in raising you, especially when you are able to see how your friends around you were brought up.

Your Time Is Precious

After you have grown up and achieved the great things you have been working tirelessly for, you will meet someone special, fall in love, and when the time is right, you'll get married and have kids of your own, which is something that people dread but are most excited about. And this is where you will get to experience what parenting is truthfully like with no filter whatsoever. But this also means you will spend less time with your own parents until their last day on Earth arrives.

This is all in the future, but for now, spend this time looking at the present. Take heed of what I say. Even though I hate to say it, you don't actually have much time left with your parents. You basically live with them for roughly eighteen years before you move out and go to college, right? Eighteen years of living with your parents is equivalent to only 6,570 days, which is 9,460,800 minutes.

If you are currently 14 years old, you have 4 years left, meaning you have a remaining 1,460 days, 2,102,400 minutes. And if you are 16 years old, you have less, leaving it at 730 days, 1,051,200 minutes. Also, you are going to have to subtract the minutes during school and any other events that keep you away from your family, but I will leave this up to your imagination. I know. Freaky, right? Remember, your time is ticking.

The same applies to grandparents. Let's be real here. You don't spend much time with them. Not to be rude, but when you were born, they were already old. And right now, they might feel lonely and not as useful since they may not have much to do, having lived their lives to the fullest back when they were young, just like what we are currently doing.

You only spend time with them for a few family dinners here and there that basically force you to be in the same room as them, or you just might never see them for a number of reasons. But remember, bad news regarding their health can easily arrive at your door, and it could take their life away as easily as you took them for granted.

Remember one thing. The passing away of your grandparents may possibly be your first time to ever grieve, and I can tell you, it strikes deep. To prevent that, the least you can do is sacrifice a few minutes of your day by calling them and checking in on how they are doing. Or you could meet up with them over coffee, pay a visit to their house, or help them cook.

My family and I took my grandparents on holiday twice a year. Traveling made them feel younger and happier, until my grandmother was suddenly diagnosed with lymphoma and gastric, colon, and brain cancer. The only thing she got out of it was weakness, which stopped her from being as active. But it never prevented her from being graceful. She still chose to put up a smile, though she woke up every day facing the fact that cancer had restrained her from doing what she loved most: cooking and baking cakes. Over time, I got busier with school. I had the chance to bake with her many times before she got sick, but I was too lazy until it was too late. And this has become one of my biggest regrets that I will forever have to live with. Don't do what I did. Instead, do the thing I failed at doing.

But today, I stand here knowing that I have learned my lesson. Just last summer, I accompanied my grandfather and walked around town with him to places he grew up in as a child. We visited places he adored, especially historical museums. He told me so much about the history of my city, Macau. I took some notes and I recorded what he said, so that if he ever forgets, I can remind him of the things he told me when we spent time together.

This is another simple yet sweet thing you can do. Take your grandparents out to brighten up their last few years of life. Cheer them up and make them smile. When you reach their age, you'll wish to have someone do the same for you. When the day of their passing comes, you'll be able to tell yourself that you did everything you could for them, and the grief won't be as overwhelming.

But do you know what spending time really means? It's not just passing a few clock hours together. It's the willingness to dedicate and sacrifice a portion of your life, however big the slice, for someone you love or care for. Spending time is something you do, not just physically, but wholeheartedly.

Our True Best Friends

Your true best friends are the people who raised you into becoming the great person you are today. Those people are what we call "family." They are the only people who will *never* abandon you, EVER. They aren't your temporary best friends in school, but your permanent best friends that will stick by your side through your ups and downs, wherever you go in life. As someone once said, "Families are like branches on a tree. We grow in different directions, yet our roots remain as one."

When you have children of your own, you would hope for them to not forget you nor abandon you. But in return, don't abandon your own parents. They are the only ones who will forever embrace you as a whole, even your flaws. They are the real love and the bond that you should mainly work on, as it completes every missing piece of your life.

Appreciate them while they are still here to receive your appreciation. Be grateful not only for all the things they have done for you but simply for their presence. Make the most of it, because something could easily happen to them tomorrow, or, who knows? Something could easily happen to you, too. Life is no guarantee. One moment, they are here, but the next, they can be gone. And so could you. You may have a lot of time on this earth, but they don't. So honor your blood so that you will never regret not doing so.

Finally, out of all the acronyms in the world, here is the best one that fits the word "FAMILY":

F - **F**ather

A - **A**nd

M - **M**other

I

L - **L**ove

Y - **Y**ou

There will be a day that you guys share the last laugh, the final hug, the final text or call, the last goodbye, and you will never see each other again. Don't let time speed by when you are present with them. Slow time down. Don't be blind and take things for granted, because one day, it may all just disappear.

"*Health is not valued till sickness comes.*"

~ Thomas Fuller

Health: The Forgotten Treasure

Have you ever watched the film or read the novel *Five Feet Apart*? Before I tell you about it, here are some biological facts. Cystic fibrosis is an inherited genetic disorder caused by the continuous production of thick mucus. This affects the respiratory and digestive system, and many other organs in the human body. CF patients tend to need a nasal cannula and, in some cases, a feeding tube (known as a G-tube) inserted into their abdomen to deliver nutrition directly to the stomach.

The story *Five Feet Apart* portrays the lives of CF patients who, aside from having a much shorter lifespan than others, must maintain a six-foot distance between themselves and other patients to prevent cross infection.

Stella Grant, a teenage girl who suffers from CF, has been living in a hospital for most of her life. But amidst everything, she remains optimistic and believes she will one day be lucky enough to recover. She makes vlogs, updating the public about her life as a CF patient, and performs her medication trial in her hospital room.

One day, Stella meets a teenage boy named Will Newman (whom she starts off disliking), who also has the same genetic disease, lives in the same hospital, and on the same floor as her. But unlike Stella, Will doesn't have much faith in recovering. So he doesn't put any effort into taking his trial medications, while there are other patients who are desperate for them. When Stella finds out about this, she makes a deal with him: to

FaceTime every day and take their medication together. They hung out more and more until they gradually fell in love, still keeping the six-foot rule in mind, which unfortunately prevents them from coming into contact with each other. But even when everything should stop them, they still break the rule in the name of love.

I have another question for you. Have you ever seen the movie or read the book *The Fault in Our Stars*? A sixteen-year-old girl named Hazel Grace Lancaster was diagnosed with metastatic thyroid cancer, which easily spread to the brain, lungs, liver, and bones. In Hazel's case, it spread to her lungs at the age of thirteen, and there hasn't been any hope for her since.

She needs a nasal cannula that is connected to an oxygen tank, which helps her breathe properly. She carries the tank everywhere she goes, at all times and at all costs. While attending a support group, she meets a boy named Augustus Waters. And like the kids in that other story, they fall in love. He then surprises her with two tickets to Amsterdam, since he really wants to make her dream of meeting her favorite author come true. And so they go. Towards the end, something happens, but hey, I won't spoil it.

So why am I sharing all this? Because the stories in those vivid films move people and help them see what it's like to be in the characters' shoes. We can empathize and understand what they're going through, even when it isn't us undergoing their struggles and feeling the pain. And this is exactly what we should be doing. Most importantly, the main message we can all take away is that we are blessed not to have to live life the way these characters do. It's easy to say that we all cherish our health, but in fact, most of us take it for granted. Movies like these awaken us to realize what a precious gift our health is.

The Gift of Life

There is one mini-exercise I do every night, which is something great to put into practice. As your day comes to an end and as you lie in bed, thank the organs in your body for functioning for yet another day, all day, and every day. Your eyes—they have seen so many beautiful things. Look at your arms and your hands. They have helped you touch and carry things. They have helped you feel and hug your loved ones. Look at your legs. Take a moment to ponder how many kilometers they have powered through all your life. But above all, your legs have helped you stand firm through everything. Look at your feet. They have helped you walk away from the darkest places.

Little things like these are worth remembering. The more you practice this five-minute exercise, the more grounded and mindful you will become of the things you do to and for your body—also of all the wonderful things your body does for you, without you even asking. You don't need to beg your heart to pump 115,200 times a day. You don't need to pump your lungs to contract and breathe 17,000 to 30,000 breaths a day. You don't even need to command your eyes to blink 28,800 times a day.

All of your bodily functions don't involve your consciousness whatsoever. You won't even notice whatever microorganisms enter your body. Even when you get a common cold or a temporary sore throat, you have 100% chance of recovering, and your body automatically does that for you. The thirty trillion cells in your body are on the grind 24/7, fighting for you every fraction of every millisecond for the rest of your life. If only you could witness that magnificence.

So the next time somebody refuses to fight for you, remember that your own body does that without you even needing to *think* about it. Other people, with poor health, are not as lucky. Their body may be failing them. So when you do catch a cold, don't even think of complaining.

At least you are lucky enough to wake up to another day, to live your life the way you want to. At least you can do the things you love without anyone stopping you. At least you don't need an oxygen tank just to breathe. Even though these are things we barely notice, they are a huge deal, and they come with a huge price. Don't think that just because we are young, we are guaranteed to live a healthy life. We aren't guaranteed anything. We're never promised to wake up tomorrow to a "regular day." This is why you need to *live* this one life you were given, today, to the fullest.

Just a couple of blocks down from where you live might be hospitals. Just setting foot into one hits a person differently, which most of the time, isn't a good vibe. The environment in a hospital completely differs from that of any other place. But the only reason why you are in there is either because of yourself or someone you care about. Either way, you would never go to a hospital if it weren't just for those two reasons.

Even if you do have to go into a hospital, you only stay there for a few hours or days until you or the person you care for recovers, while some people are required to spend much longer there. There is a possibility that in rooms on every floor, people of all ages, young and old, may be terminally ill or obliged to live their lives inside hospital rooms and on hospital beds—especially when they can't survive without advanced medical treatment which is confined to hospitals only. And so they are forever stuck in there, whether they like it or not. Getting out and having the opportunity to move around and see the world with your own eyes is the best and most incredible feeling ever. But there are millions of people in the same world we live in, who don't have the ability to enjoy that simple pleasure. But most of us are given this gift.

These thoughts really hit me when my mom's friend, who had cancer, approached me, and out of nowhere, asked "Can I hug you?" Of course, I accepted the hug, but the feeling I got was overwhelming. The fact that she was battling cancer yet she was always smiling brightly, and was more joyful than many who are healthy, made me reflect on the gift of life. When she hugged me, the thought that I wasn't the one who had the cancer growing in me made me feel sorrow, but gratefulness at the same time. This was a true eye-opener.

Many people don't get to decide how they want to live their lives because their health condition sets them back and makes the decision for them. They have to fight their own war of survival. It's a battlefield out there every single second, not knowing whether it will be their last. Others aren't so lucky to make it, even when everything seemed fine just a few seconds before. And if you are one of the lucky ones to recover from a severe illness, you have a miracle story to tell, and your voice will always be heard.

The Day the Tables Turn

It certainly is a sobering thought that one can be healthy this moment but things could easily go wrong the next when you least expect it to, no matter what age you are, wherever you are. Even if you are in perfect shape and excellent condition right now.

In addition to this, there's one thing most teens don't fathom completely. Have you ever done something that could easily trigger health risks or ruin your entire life just because it made you feel somewhat cool? Made you feel you could run away from your problems? Come on, we all know I'm talking about drugs, smoking, and alcohol. This is what I like to call "the Big Three." But in the end, they aren't so big after all.

Don't lie to yourself. Have you ever smoked a joint? Or drunk anything that you already knew could ruin your young and healthy life, yet you still did it for the sake of fun? Teens tend to value popularity and trends more than things that benefit them. If you know you have done these things, I would like to ask you two questions: how can a person be so foolish? And have you forgotten that the druggy products you use may not expire, but you will? When the short-lived fun is over, there is nothing you can get out of these experiences apart from regret—nothing more, and nothing can change that.

This was confirmed for me when a group of friends I knew went out and got themselves incredibly drunk the weekend before exams. While hungover before an exam early the next morning, one person from that group sat next to me, admitting how stupid she felt. "I should have thought twice. It was a mistake"—that sort of classic excuse. She started tearing up, telling me how disappointed her mom was when she found out. She even went so far as to say she would never be able to live with herself, knowing she had made that one, dumb decision.

I was mainly shocked because this girl had always been that bright intellectual and athletic person in school, and just that one decision she'd made turned her whole world upside down. This proves one thing: all it takes is one wrong brick to send a whole building collapsing into pieces. High chance it may never be rebuilt as greatly as it was before—which in this case, was her reputation.

Most importantly, if you're using the Big Three to alleviate any pain or struggles you are facing, that is just pathetic. Are you so weak that you can't find a realistic way to cope? Come on. You are better than that. And if you classify this as fun, it ain't real. You don't need to drink and smoke to have fun, unless you believe having liver disease or lung cancer is enjoyable. These "fun" things are a distraction from the serious consequences you will face after your "fun" is over. The pleasure you get out of getting wasted and high is only temporary. Remember the girl I just mentioned, who turned out to be a huge letdown and disgrace to her family.

Worst of all, if you do these things, you are just indirectly killing yourself, damaging millions of healthy cells and killing a healthy body that other people would die to have. It may not happen all at once, but do you really want to be trapped in a body that's full of suffering when you reach your thirties or forties? If you even make it that far. You're going to be stuck in this body for the rest of your life, so it's not smart to break the machinery.

This was proven when I received some news that one of my childhood friends OD'd and was found dead overnight in his apartment, at the age of sixteen. When I found out, the first thing I thought of was his smile and how goofy he was when we were little kids. He was a talented and gifted musician who was full of life, but it was all taken away from him. This news really was an eye-opener for everyone. There were rumors that he had been mentally struggling, but all I could think of was the saying: "I would rather listen to your problems than attend your funeral." It's so disheartening when perfectly healthy people would rather harm themselves, even when they face problems that could be solved if they spoke about them.

If you take drugs, remember that you could be the next victim. All this says about you is that you clearly don't know how to value yourself. You don't see how irreplaceable your health is. In the end, your health is way more important than the losers who pressure you to abuse it. Your health is something you definitely don't want to screw up.

Moral of the story, folks: make the most of everything you are given in this lifetime. Make the wisest decisions on how you are going to spend your healthy, beautiful, and bright days ahead. It shouldn't take a pandemic to make us realize the importance of this.

Chapter Three: Peers, Who Are They Really?

*"It's better to walk alone than with a
crowd going in the wrong direction."*

~ Diane Grant

Friendships, peer pressure, and bullying—I had a rough time with them all, mainly due to my skin condition. In kindergarten, children were already making fun of me. I always knew what made it hard for me to fit in, since I displayed something that made me stand out so much. As I grew older, I experienced peer pressure to change who I was as a person in order for people to "accept" me. But when I refused to change, people said even more horrible things about my physical appearance.

Many spread false rumors about me, intending to ruin others' perceptions of me and to end the friendships I most cherished. And because of this, I lost the greatest of friends along the way. Even when I did have a few friends, they wouldn't stay for long because their views of me were easily clouded by the manipulation of others. If you were known to be my friend, you would get bullied alongside me, which was the crappiest part. Many people feared that, so they tended to run. Either way, people rarely stayed.

The more cunning ones used me to be their friend as their last option when they were scared of being alone, and once they amended things with their old friends, they would leave me to go back to them. When I was thirteen, I was hissed at in class and on that same day, body-shamed face-to-face by boys.

Now, if you are someone who is quick to judge anyone who doesn't look like you do, allow me to say just one thing. Don't *ever* judge someone who was born different. They are already going through a much harder time than everyone else, so try not to make it worse than it already is for them.

For me, as someone who has a skin condition, it was hard to even wear short sleeves and shorts outside without being glared at. I hid to the point where I was even willing to wear long sleeves during the summer. This was why every year, I was desperately waiting for winter to arrive, so that I could hide and look normal for once. To this very day, I haven't worn shorts out in public, but I am now opening up to that option. But for you, you don't even have to think about this because your skin is clear. I did all of this to hide who I truly was because I thought that if no one would accept me for me, then I couldn't accept me either.

I doubted myself and didn't have the courage to get myself out of those negative thoughts. I became distant from everything and everyone and stopped doing the things I loved. The biggest and most valuable thing I lost was myself. I lost faith in who I was because of the belief that I had nothing left. And if I am not mistaken, this may be exactly how you feel, too.

I'm not saying all this to play the victim or for you to pity me. I don't need that, and don't want that from you. All I want to say is that people are going through tough times behind shut doors. My reason for sharing my story is so others can have someone to relate to, and so this can perhaps encourage them to share their own story of strength. I also tell you my story because I am proud of how far I have come.

In your case, you might have gone through something along these lines in your life, and I am here for you. All I hope is for you to regain yourself through these next few pages. On the other hand, if you have been blessed enough to not experience this, you might think that people like me are somewhat unfortunate. In a way, you aren't wrong. Yes, the experience is crap, but the outcome of the journey is completely and entirely worth it. I have grown to believe that everyone is lucky enough to go through tough times that hold so many key things that we should all learn and never forget. After all, if I didn't go through all of that, I wouldn't be here helping you.

The Life Cycle of a Butterfly

After all of my experiences, the first thing I gathered is that it's better to avoid constantly concentrating on what is happening *to* you. Instead, flip your mindset and put your focus on what you can actually learn from all this. The only thing you really need to keep in mind through everything is that the process only consists of two parts: the bad news and the good news. Bad news is, you are hurting because you are growing. But the good news is, you are growing because you are hurting—which is the turning point for a better change. It takes a while to understand this, but once you give it some thought, you will know that it's *all* in the process of self-growth, which takes time.

You are shedding your skin. The old skin you are growing out of is the old you. It will hurt, but the person that you are becoming is someone who is more worthy to hurt for.

Even if the phase may be ugly, the end result is absolutely beautiful. You are becoming the better and greater person you are destined to be in your own unique way, even when people intentionally strive to give you pain. You are like a caterpillar, coming out of its chrysalis to emerge, in the end, as a magnificent butterfly.

You are learning new things that you have never learned about yourself before, and they are things worth valuing, even when they aren't noticed by others. Plus, you will need to learn how to love those things at one point in life anyway, now or later. So, might as well save time and do it now, right?

With that in mind, I began to earn everything back over time, and in the end, the greatest thing I regained was myself. Most of all, I learned to not let go of what makes me who I am. I learned to have courage, to love and embrace my physical appearance. I learned how to celebrate the beautiful and unique patterns on every inch of my skin. I mean, how cool is it to naturally be born tatted? I couldn't be proud of anything greater.

I get to witness the elegant way my patterns shift and fade over time, and I love that piece of me. And hey, I grew to end up with the greatest success I have today. From losing friends and spending days alone to cultivating true friendship, the whole process helped me eliminate specific people who would never benefit me in any way. It was better to lose those people now than later. Thankfully, I now have a small group of real and true friends who respect and cherish our friendship. And of course, I have my family by my side 24/7.

Now, during your own experiences, one thing to remember is that in these situations, the biggest mistake you could ever make is beating yourself up and doubting life in general. What I want you to ask yourself is, "What can I learn from this?" instead of "What did I do to deserve this?" And that is exactly where the game changes. Most of the time, we want to change the situation, but sometimes we need to let the circumstances change *us* for the better. Over time, you will eventually overcome the challenge you face with your own power and will. It always depends on your mindset. Just like they say: "A storm won't last forever."

"A real friend is one who walks in when
the rest of the world walks out."

~ Walter Winchell

Friends. Oh, the joy of friends! Reading that single word may make you think of someone or of a few people who are genuinely on your side. Or it may be the opposite. Maybe what rushed through your mind was something complicated, or a dark place you would rather not visit.

It's normal for your mind to wander around and feed you questions like, "Why don't I have any friends? Why do my "friends" end up going behind my back even when I trusted them with every single thing? Do people not like me? Am I not good enough? Do I fit in? Have I done something? Or do I just need to change something about myself?"

If you are there, in that place alone, what you need to know is that God ended a lot of toxic friendships that you wanted to keep forever. You can't ever control whether people stay or not. Whoever is meant to be by your side will certainly stay. Plus, it's better to have no one than have the wrong ones. Most importantly, surround yourself with those who see your worth instead of with those who (intentionally or not) make you feel lonely even when you are in a crowd. The only way you can ever flourish is by identifying who treats you this way and cutting them off. Save yourself, your time, and your energy, and invest them in things that are actually worth saving. In the end, you'll never be lonely. You have yourself, and you'll have yourself until you die. Go save *that* person.

The Truth about Friendships

We all know that friendships surely aren't all about sleepovers, pillow fights, butterflies, and rainbows, because in reality, it's rarely like that. But what *is* a real friend? When I ask that basic question, you might be going, "Uh… Well, that's easy. I can answer that." But for the deep thinkers out there (like me), you might have thought deeper than the surface—which is exactly what we need. Either way, pause and take this time to think of your own definition of a "real friend."

Don't start doubting or thinking about whether your friends are real or not. Forget about them for a minute. The only thing you need to think of at the moment are the key factors that make up your ideal friend. Aim to become that person, so that you can attract the same in someone else.

A lot of people don't actually take time to think about the kind of friend they *need*. Instead, they waste time on the wrong people just because they are *already there*. Sadly, some do this because they either "don't have a choice" or because they are pressured into being friends with anyone available so that they won't appear as lonely to others. If this is you, you may have brought it on yourself by encouraging those pointless friendships. Or maybe they just happened without your meaning for them to.

Now think about the people you surround yourself with. Are they any good to you? Are they *real*? By surrounding yourself with the wrong people, you can easily become blind to who is real and who isn't. If worse comes to worst, you will eventually turn out just like them, which of course, won't end well.

This is why I would rather stick to quality than quantity. I personally prefer having a smaller group of wise and real friends who share the same values as me, who spread positive energy, and who have pure intentions. You should be able to see your friends as role models, who have a good influence on you and the way you function. The friends you have should reflect the person you want to turn out like, whether you admire them because of their work ethic, their passion for great things, their attitude when they stand and deal with obstacles, or some other great quality. People who don't empower you to improve yourself as a person or deliver any of the above aren't worth making friends with. So stick to those who *are* worth it.

I would rather have a small friendship group of quality people, than a huge group of bad influences, gossipers, drug addicts, smokers, and party freaks—basically people who aren't at all the best to hang out with since day one. You need to identify which of the above is your friendship group. If you aren't finding peace there, it's a sign that you don't belong there. This is where you then need to distinguish whether people are being friends with you because they value who you are, or because they want something from you. There is a huge difference between the two. It can easily be spotted if you are attentive enough. It can also easily be ignored, because not many people pay enough attention to notice the fine line.

Getting Accepted into a Peer Group

Many foolish people openly flex their wealth. By showing off how rich they are, they attract people, not because they are friend quality, not because they have a good personality, and not because they are attractive.

But funnily enough, their bank account is. And these people are blind enough to spend their wealth buying their entry ticket into friendships. If this is what you do, or if you know people who are like that, I hope you realize the consequences.

This will only attract the wrong things, the wrong people, along with their wrong intentions. This isn't the way to win sincere friends. Others will use you to get something from you for free, like money or illicit things like drugs and alcohol. Or they might hang out with you to gain fame and popularity. If you are treated like this, you need to understand that they are only using you to upgrade their status at school. If people do this around you, this is where it all goes terribly wrong, not for them, but for you.

Even though it seems that being popular is a good thing, you should reconsider, because all people will see when they look at you is a source of fame or money, and this is why they are always sticking to you. This will only end up with them not cherishing you as a friend, but only using you. To prevent this, set some boundaries or just leave them. And regarding money, perhaps you should become more private with your spending. It's about time, isn't it?

Now think about yourself. Do you hang out with your friends because you share a genuine and inseparable bond with them? Are *you* the one who is using *them* for popularity, money, etc.? This is where the reverse card is played.

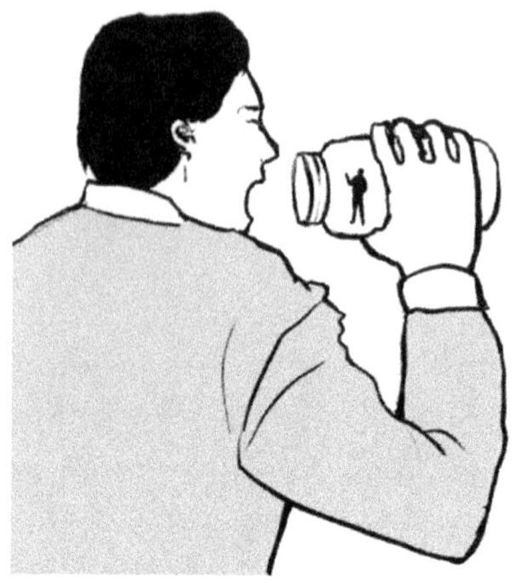

*"You never really see how toxic someone
is until you breathe fresher air."*

Going back to the first question about your ideal friend, it's kind of sad to say, but few teens are observant enough to see what they want in a friend. Even if they get the idea of what a real friend is, most teens don't act like one, or they are just caught up in toxic friendships without realizing. This leads to what I am going to say next. I'm going to list the things that a real friend *doesn't* do:

1) A real friend doesn't lie

If a friendship is open and genuine, the friends don't deal in lies. They have no reason to be false with each other. It's stupid to think you're a friend if you lie behind your friend's back. You don't deserve to keep that friendship. Be smart enough to know that if you lie, your friend will probably find out from another person. And when they do, their views on you will completely change, and, if they're smart, they will end up dropping you.

To prevent this, always try to be as truthful and honest as possible. The more you lie, the more impure and untrue your friendship becomes with the other person. This leads to trust issues, insecurity and instability in the friendship. Plus, you might get lied to in return, which would really suck.

2) A real friend doesn't backstab

Backstabbing is a killer. It's a horrible thing to betray someone, and it sure isn't pleasant to have someone backstab *you* in return. By backstabbing, you show that you're weak and are trying to hide your own insecurities, at someone else's expense. This is cruel. It truly shows who is superior, and in this case, it's definitely not you.

So don't start badmouthing your friend just because one small thing happened. People tend to spread each other's secrets after falling out, but be wise enough to have your mouth sealed at all times, no matter how big the problem. You need to be strong and capable of dealing with problems on your own, and of course, you shouldn't function by running your mouth anyway. Don't let your emotions control the words that come out of your mouth. You need to control what you say and just shut up before you are told to shut up.

When you "spill the tea," you need to be careful of where you spill it, because tea stains, and it stays there forever. The best thing to do is keep it to yourself, but if you are desperate to gossip about someone, choose wisely. The best person or people to resort to are your parents, because I guarantee you, they will never backstab you. Remember that gossip always unleashes the inner bitch in everyone, so you need to be cautious who you expose to that side of you.

Some people have the audacity to create a private Instagram or Snapchat story just to badmouth others. It really is daft, and targeting people on social media is literally cyberbullying. How important does someone have to be for you to create an account and post stuff about them on your story?

If you aren't the one talking trash, note that there will be a time when people will ask you about your side of the situation. I've had my fair share of weird people talking trash about me to my face, listing all the things that they hate about me. It sure is absurd, and if you've never had to deal with such pure idiocy, then you are a very lucky person.

If your so-called "friends" do this, they are not mature enough to know what requires their comment and what doesn't. They will still go around running their mouths, whether you like it or not. In the end, that is the only thing they are good at.

Over the years, they won't be able to keep up their façade. Even if they put on a show on the outside, in time their true colors will start to be noticed. The best part is, other people will start realizing who they really are and will vow to themselves to stay as far away as possible.

This is because fake people who backstab are hard to be around. After a ton of gossiping and ranting, they're simply a huge bore. Whatever comes out of their mouth isn't worth hearing, and no one will have much fun with them.

It reminds me of what Brian Tracy said in *Eat That Frog!*: "Refuse to complain about your problems. Keep them to yourself. As speaker/humorist Ed Foreman says, 'You should never share your problems with others because 80% of the people don't care about them anyway, and the other 20% are kind of glad that you've got them in the first place.'" I couldn't help but giggle when I read that.

If you are a gossiper, it's time to get real. Spreading gossip doesn't solve your insecurity. In all honesty, it only makes you seem pathetic. Try to not be a gossiping entertainer, because it really is tiring. You're just putting on a façade to entertain a crowd who barely cares about your "juicy" gossip. Now, this is my gossip for *you*. You put on this mask because you're ashamed of yourself. You're afraid people will notice how weak, vulnerable, and insecure you really are. But people can see right through you. So word of advice, quit being such a phony.

Pay close attention to the way your friends gossip about others. If your friends don't gossip much, that's wonderful. But if your friends are the bitchiest in town, that's bad news for you, because it will surely be the way they talk about you. Whatever you've opened up to them about, they'll eventually use against you as a weapon, and all your secrets will be spilled. They may be your friends today but can change their minds tomorrow. Even if they gossip only about small things, they will surely have a lot to say about you if something goes wrong with the friendship all of a sudden. But amidst all this, you must remember that some people will try to expose what is wrong with you because they can't stand what is right about you.

If you are the one spreading things about someone you had a quarrel with, once your friendship is amended with that person, you still run the risk of other people telling that friend what you said about them, back when you were not on good terms. All of your hurtful words can come around the corner and bite you back, probably ending your friendship for good. Also, this says so much about you as a human being. Is that the kind of person you truly want to be? Someone no one can count on? A betrayer?

Victory always goes to the one who hasn't said a single bad thing, because the most powerful thing you can say in situations like these, is nothing at all. If someone is flooding you with gossip about a friend they just broke off with, don't let it spread. Don't let a single word escape your mouth, because next time around, they will be the one to backstab *you*. Don't be a fool.

3) A real friend isn't petty

Pettiness basically translates to insecurity. Being petty only results in you focusing on the little, negative, and unnecessary things that no one else even thinks about. This could mean that you may also overthink and imagine things that aren't as bad as you believe, putting you in conflict with yourself, which is mentally unhealthy.

Just let it go, man. It's all locked in your own imagination. Tiny things shouldn't matter anyway. They will only keep eating away at your thoughts if you don't put an end to the habit. It's quite frankly toxic.

Don't be that petty person who gives a little shove to an ex-friend when you pass them by, or who arrogantly rolls their eyes when they're in the same room. If you think that will make a difference to them, it won't, because you don't mean much to them by now, so don't act as if you do.

In short, pettiness is childish. If a friendship ends for you, deal with it with some dignity. Don't make yourself small over it. Don't waste your time doing stupid things you will probably regret a year from now. Resolve to be bigger than that.

4) A real friend isn't manipulative

Manipulation is when one will do anything in their power to tear down someone who they see as superior to them. Many people backstab, not only with gossip, but with manipulation to turn others against a person they envy or resent. If you are a person who behaves this way, you are the one who needs fixing up, because you're the most damaged.

Just keep your devious ways to yourself and stop trying to make other people's lives so much more difficult than they already are. Perhaps you should try to get your own life together instead of trying to ruin someone else's. You are stopping yourself from getting on with your own life and reaching your own happiness because you are so occupied thinking about destroying others. Like for real though, what is your purpose? Even better, what is your problem? Bad-mouthing, backstabbing, gossiping, and manipulating are cheap ways of putting the spotlight on other people, in hopes that no one will notice your own inadequacies.

If you have beef with someone, don't be that manipulative person who gets a huge army involved in your business. Don't be toxic enough to say, "I don't want you getting involved" to your gossiping crew, when the truth is you want them to do your dirty work. If you don't want them involved, why are you telling them every detail about what happened? If you really don't want people involved, then why are you involving them? Don't hint or outright ask others to gang up on someone you are mad at. If that's how you entertain yourself, I feel very sorry for you.

If you're someone who's lost friends because someone has manipulated them into leaving you, kiss them goodbye, because they don't deserve an inch of you. The reason they left you during those dark times is because they made a choice. They chose to listen to what others had to say about you instead of trusting their own experience with you and their own judgment. You don't need that kind of turncoat in your life.

The person doing all the manipulating wants to have more people on their side just to go against you. This shows who the stronger person really is. It's you, because in order to defeat you, they need a whole army of people on their side. Just remain blessed and unbothered without them. People can step out of your life as easily as they stepped in. As someone once said, "Fake friends are no different than shadows. They stick around during your brightest moments, but disappear during your darkest hours."

Don't let people's judgment of a friend of yours cloud your own opinion of that person. Trust your own experience with that friend. Don't fall for the trap, because if someone is targeting your friend, most of what you hear about them will probably be made up. Assume that the gossip you hear is as fake as the person who told you.

5) A real friend doesn't hold grudges

Holding grudges is a waste of time. It's also a waste of energy and is toxic to you and those around you. All that clung-to anger does you no good. If you get a reputation as a grudge holder, people will keep their distance because they'll want nothing to do with you.

Whatever people have done to you, don't hate them for eternity. The other person has probably forgotten about what happened between you guys, so there is no excuse for you to hold on. The more you nurture grudges from the past, the more you *live* in the past. The longer you hold onto a grudge, the more it's going to dominate your life. You must let it go, heal, move on, work on yourself, and start living life for yourself. If you held onto every single bad thing you have ever encountered in life, how could you possibly breathe?

Reflecting on Yourself and Others

Well, I hope this summed things up well enough for you to self-reflect on the type of friend you are today, and especially on those you surround yourself with. If your friends do all the listed things, just keep in mind that they're fake, and that there will be much greater friends on offer for you.

The reason why your friendships might constantly be ending is simply because you are growing. You are different from the person you were when you became friends with those people back then. People grow apart, and it's normal. It's impossible to maintain every single friendship with every single friend since day one. You will lose a lot of people here and there along the journey of life and self-discovery. It's growth. It's natural.

There will be people willing to accept and love you for you, and that is an incredible thing. When they do, don't abuse that. Appreciate those underrated people who are willing to make a huge difference in your life, because not many people have a heart like that.

So before you leave school for good, before you get a job and settle down, look around you and remember those who treated you right even when others didn't. And when you have finally gained success in life, remember that they were the ones who helped you get there.

Like with family, there will come a day when you and your friends share the last laugh, the final hug, the final text or call, the final goodbye, and you will never see each other again. People drift apart. One day, your children will point at a picture of you with your friends, and ask, "Who are they?" You will simply smile down and say, "They were the ones who I shared the best days of my life with." You will relive that moment, remembering that they were the individuals who made your old days rock.

Now, my challenge for you is to do the same. Be a generous friend with a pure heart. Be that person who will choose to make a difference in people's lives. Smile when you walk past other people, and I guarantee you, they will smile back, and that is an exchange of positivity. Even this will make a difference and can make someone's day. You may have saved them from having a bad day or being sad. Choose to sit next to someone when they are sitting alone in class or on the bus. Choose to compliment others and make them happy, maybe for the first time in a long time. Choose to make a positive impact on those around you.

We are all viewed differently by the different people who know us. You could be the mysterious stranger who walked into a coffee shop this morning. You could be seen as the smartass in class. You could be a really attractive person from afar. You could be a villain in someone's life. You could be that sporty person someone looks up to. You could be the lonely and quiet one who sits in the corner of the bus.

We are one person, but viewed through different lenses in other people's minds. When you put the effort into becoming a better person to others, you will become a better person to yourself as well. And when you treat others well, there will always be someone who will do the same for you. After all, you get what you give. If you spread positivity and happiness, you will get that or even more in return. All you need to do is make sure you are remembered as the best person possible. We will never know what people are going through behind those closed doors. It takes zero dollars to be nice to someone and put a smile on their face. There is no cost and no expense to it, yet some people would still rather not. Behavior comes with a choice. Sadly, lots of people don't make the right one.

*"When you say 'yes' to others, make sure
you don't say 'no' to yourself."*

~ Paulo Coelho

Let's talk about peer pressure. It's something unavoidably dangerous. I have never actually experienced a ton of it myself, but it's true that a lot of teenagers and adults experience this nowadays. Teen or adult, the pressure varies and ranges, and the extremities depend a lot on the person who undergoes it.

This mainly depends on your response to the influences around you. Let's take swearing as an example. You might not swear, but being surrounded by friends who do will cause you to get into the same habit after a while. Why? Because your friends do it, so you do it. That's not exactly peer pressure. It's more like mindlessly going with the herd. We've all had that experience. I guess that's how peer pressure works, too, but on a different level.

Don't Lie to Yourself

If you know that your friends are bad influences, maintain a distance or leave them before you get any further involved in their business. They could easily pressure you into fitting in or even doing irreversible things to prove your worth. They might have already done it. Most kids make the mistake of ignoring these facts and continue hanging out with their sorry friends because they tell themselves, "Oh, I would *never* do what my friends are doing. I will *never* be like them." But no matter how many times you say that to yourself, you will end up being manipulated, and eventually you will give in. You'll begin to do the things they do, because their behavior will start to feel familiar, and what feels familiar starts to feel acceptable and normal.

Don't downgrade yourself. If you're going to change, resolve to change not for the worse, but the better. The influences around you can easily have an effect on everything in your life, so be careful what you expose yourself to and who you hang out with. Things can easily get out of hand, which only happens once you let others control your decisions for you. After something bad happens, you'll blame yourself for your mistake, but it will be too late. The joke ends up being on you, because life will demand that you pay the price for your misguided behavior.

Of course I could tell you that you can always easily say no, and you will think saying no sounds extremely easy. But it's not easy when you're in the situation. So stay out of the situation in the first place. I know a lot of people, especially girls, who have been pressured into doing things that they never wanted or planned to do, knowing all along that they could have said no at the time.

They ended up saying yes. They felt obliged to do things because they feared they'd be looked down upon if they walked away. So instead of standing tall, they got themselves into serious trouble. No one forced them to get involved with those kids or to make *their* dream of "fun" come true. But to be accepted, they had to discard something precious about themselves. That's how peer pressure works.

For what purpose are you trying to fit in? Is there someone you are trying to satisfy? Do you feel a need to blend in with the "popular" crowd that wanders through the corridors of school? If that's you, ask yourself this excellent question from life coach Vex King: "Are you doing what makes you happy or are you doing what will make you feel accepted? Don't confuse real happiness with validation from others."

Don't ever try to make others happy at the expense of yourself. Most of us (myself included) feel pressured to always be outgoing and happy, not to ruin other people's good moods. I fake being happy sometimes because I don't like being seen as someone negative and depressing. But faking what we're feeling can be damaging and draining to our happiness. We just have to accept that we won't always be in a great state and that it's okay to have a bad day from time to time.

You won't get far in life if you are always trying to please others by trying to meet their expectations of you. If you live by others' standards and expectations, you'll never find peace being your true self. Most importantly, you will completely forget who you truly are, because it's almost impossible to be yourself around people who have different perspectives of you. Refuse to follow others, and go for better options. You need to make peace with your own environment. And when you do, I promise you, it will be the best decision you ever made, because you saved yourself by going solo instead of compromising who you are just so you could blend in.

Understand Your Worth

The reason why some kids feel a desperate need to fit in is because they either haven't seen their own uniqueness yet or because they are scared to stand alone. Get yourself out of that mental state, and be friends with people who are actually worth it. If you keep adapting to the influences of your surroundings, you'll waste time trying to fit in with the wrong crowd.

So let me tell you one thing that will save you from wasting time: fitting in with the wrong crowd is the *last* thing you want to do. The more you try, the more you will stand out. If you change yourself every single time other people want you to, you will never catch up, and you'll never find peace within yourself. You'll only feel even more insecure. Your self-confidence, your views on everything, your relationships, and your performance will all take a hit. You'll feel lost, not knowing who you are or if you even have value. Don't let this be you.

"Birds of a feather flock together"—so goes the old saying. It means that people with the same personality, intentions, and influences hang out and bunch together in their own groups. For example, if you aren't a gossiper and if you try to fit into a gossiping group, it won't work, honey. If you are not a druggy, you wouldn't fit into a druggy environment, right? You may be worried that you'll never find a group that you can click with, but set your standards high, be willing to go it alone, and in time you'll find and attract others like yourself. Don't be dumb enough to do anything it takes just to get in with a group.

Set some boundaries and standards of what you will accept from others. Don't stress out and force yourself to be friends with people you don't really like. The more you desperately seek friendships, the more you will attract those who aren't meant for you. The reason why you are struggling to fit in is simply because you don't belong there. You belong somewhere greater. Sticking to these people will cause a personality morph, so you better get yourself out of there before you literally turn into them or something much worse. Once you do, there is no going back, which reminds me of the people I grew up with, and how those same childhood best friends have ended up. I lost most of them because we had completely different interests. They preferred alcohol over friendships.

You see, no matter how much you change yourself, you will still get judged, so don't bother. There will always be people who will not be happy with your decisions based on whatever you want to do, however and whenever. At the end of the day, it's best to have people hate you for who you are than love you for something you aren't. Plus, you will never be able to please every person you encounter.

This is one reason why it's better to have a smaller group of friends. If you're friends with a herd of people, it will be difficult to make time for yourself to think, grow, and self-recharge, since you are tirelessly busy pleasing everyone around you. Everyone will have different levels of respect for you, but the most important respect you can receive is from yourself. Love, respect, and embrace the true person you are on the inside, not the fake person you are tempted to display around others.

Be Kind to Yourself

Yes, you read that right. Do it. Treat yourself the way you would treat a friend. Make peace; hang out with yourself until you eventually realize what you deserve. This way, you will know what type of friend you essentially need in life, and you will be friends with those who will treat you the way you treat yourself.

You shouldn't even care about what others think of you. You do you, and as long as you try to be a better person for yourself, you have earned success in your own way, and no one can tell you otherwise. Once you have discovered your true self and where you stand, their opinions of you won't matter at all. Once you have found the inner peace within you, you will be the first to find eternal joy.

This is why saying no takes a lot of courage. If you were strong enough to say no before, you can do it again. But remember, even if you said it once, you can easily give in and say yes the next time around. Some believe that saying yes makes you tough, but it's actually the other way round. Saying no is what really makes you tough, because you are willing to stand alone by your decision when others would huddle together because of their wimpy fear of sticking out and looking different. Individually, they are all too weak to say no, but in unity, they say yes to appear strong.

People bunch together just to lure you into thinking that your decision isn't right. But at the end of the day, if you get picked on or made fun of for "chickening out" after making the right decision, stand proud, leave the group, and be happy about it. They will one day see who was right. After all, if they get into trouble, at least you weren't there to get involved.

To become strong on your own, you need to wake up and start owning up to your personal standards, because you know better than any group what is best for yourself and how to protect yourself from harm. You should never feel the need to do things that you don't want to do just so you can please others and be accepted into a peer group. If that is how you make friends, you don't know how to sustain your own validation of yourself. The only way people can be your true friends is by accepting what you do based on your *own* decisions. Real friends would never pressure you to do anything.

A good rule of thumb is don't do anything you wouldn't want your parents to find out about or witness. Keep this in mind. If your friends try to get you to join in the "fun" by saying they will look out for you, note that in reality, no one will put the effort into keeping you safe. If something unexpected happens, such as an accident or someone passing out or getting arrested, they will all prioritize themselves first, even when they promised to take care of you. Who would ever put anyone else first in this type of situation? No one. They will run for their lives while you stand there, *defenseless.*

Next time, debate with yourself about whether what you're thinking of doing is right. When the time comes to decide whether you will risk your life doing stupid and reckless things, just pause and remember this: whatever happens to your future self can be the result of what you are doing to yourself right now.

Whatever you are about to do, do it for and because of yourself and no one else. What happens next is your responsibility, and it will only happen to *you.* If you think doing bad things is your ticket to adulthood, then you are going to have to think again. All it proves is how irresponsible you are. Independence only comes in the package if you are someone who is wise, who thinks independently, and does things that will only *benefit* you and lift you up.

If you do something harmful because you think you are "grown up" or "mature enough," you might as well be classified as dependent, since you are incapable of naturally and instinctively making the right decisions for yourself. You are just growing up in reverse.

People like this come running back, crying to mommy when plans take a turn for the worse. Just know it was your own fault all along, because you should have known and done better. At the end of the day, you were the one who let this happen to yourself. You will never be able to take back your actions or reverse the situation. There is no going back. Your entire life can be ruined by one stupid mistake you made decades ago.

To the bullies:

*"Stealing stars out of someone else's sky
won't make yours shine any brighter."*

~ Samantha de Senna Fernandes

Bullies, if you are reading this, you are not liked AT ALL. Yes, it's in CAPS. Hear me say it through these pages. If there is a willingness for change within you, have at it. If you see no reason to improve yourself as a person for those around you, then please at least do it for yourself.

The Unspoken Vulnerability

If we're going to talk about bullies, let's start with some basic facts. Bullies don't exist without three things: fakeness, toxicity, and insecurity. Bullies have a growing obsession of desperately needing to be accepted. This makes people do terrible things that they never dreamt of doing, just to appear more powerful and entitled than others—even though deep down, they know they aren't, and nothing can change that. This is why they can't stop.

I have always despised bullies since day one, and of course, I was despised in return. But note that those who have tried to interfere with my life have learned their lesson not to mess with someone like me. I don't care whether you think you are a good person behind your villain instincts, and I don't care whether you think you are liked by the whole world. Behind your back, your "friends" say what they truly think of you.

If you ask any adult, they will all say the same thing: that bullies seemed so tough back when they were teenagers. But after the bullies left school and attempted careers of their own, then showed up for a class reunion some years later, everyone noticed how most of them turned out to be a "nobody." They became lame and unsuccessful, and their status totally downgraded. No one expected them to end up that way because of how much power they used to show off, but beneath all their villainy, they were weak.

Bullies are commonly known for being the most blind to the damage they have wrought. If you're a bully, you might not be in total control of your actions and might not even see that you are constantly doing terrible things with full intentions of harming those around you. If you haven't noticed who you have become over the years, look at yourself. Reflect, and realize what you look like through other people's eyes.

We have all done some type of bullying at least once in our life, or purposely did something small to make someone annoyed or to lower their self-esteem. And yes, the feeling you get out of it is great, and you may feel completely fine because well, you're not the one who is suffering. This is why people are easily addicted to bullying. It's like a trampoline. You jump, it lowers the springs, then you bounce high. You come back down and jump again and again, higher and higher, until you are eventually tired.

The springs in this case are other people's self-esteem. When you jump, the springs lower, and you bounce higher each time, meaning that their self-esteem keeps on lowering when yours only gets higher, making you end up in a higher position than them. And when you fall back down, this makes you jump higher each time to beat the height you reached last time. Once you get tired of jumping up and down, the springs are worn out and broken like the feelings of the people you caused harm to.

You might have assumed that you are bigger, cooler, or somehow superior to everyone else, right? But what you don't know is, you're caught up in your own illusion. You are just as lonely as those you bully, but you don't want people to know that. So you try to make others feel bad so you don't feel alone. You fear being the victim, and that's why you became the bully.

Picking on others, and making them feel insecure like you, makes you feel more entitled. Do you now know how appalling this behavior is? You are scarring and making your mark on other people's lives, forever. You will always be remembered as the horrible kid who made people's teenage years so much more miserably complicated than they had to be. That is the only thing you'll be remembered for in the record books.

If you think about it, the "nerds," the "unpopular" kids, or anyone you have put down in the past, are the ones who will end up rising higher than you ever will. In reality, they might already be in a higher position than you. Trying to drag people down suggests that you are already inferior to them. You are angry and possibly envious that you don't have what they have. You can't accept it, and you're heartless, so you attack. You thrive on killing happiness instead of on finding your own. And this is why I truly pity you, because your only shot at your poor version of "happiness" is at the expense of others.

You can already see that they are more successful than you, and that's why you steal their sparkle. You literally have nothing else to live for apart from trying to steal it. You see the light and joy in them that you never see yourself having. You can clearly see that your victims are EVERYTHING great that you aren't. Yeah, the word EVERYTHING is in CAPS, too. You are constantly giving them battles to fight every day, and they are constantly growing, which only makes them stronger by the second, thanks to you, by the way.

Once they have reached their destined place in life, all they will do is thank you for your help in getting them there. One day you will look up to those you have looked down upon, and feel nothing but ashamed of yourself, because all along you were motivating them to become something greater and to earn their rightful place in society. And once they do, they will cherish their accomplishments, and laugh at the memory of your pathetic tricks. This is what I call, "future payback."

Bullying Isn't the Answer

But what if someone has been mean to you in the past? Should you attempt to get even now, and bully them back? Even if people have done wrong to you in the past, bullying them in return is never a good answer. That just lowers you to their miserable level. It's in the past anyway, and it's best to leave it at that. Everyone around you is living their own lives, actually getting things done. Don't be the one to live in the past, stewing over past wrongs and nursing your old scars.

So bullies, here's a question for you: do you really feel better by picking on someone for something that they can't change about themselves? Their physical appearance, their looks, their IQ, their race, or whatever? I'm pretty sure that *you* are more self-conscious of these categories than the actual people you've been bullying. I bet you don't really have much to say about them and just choose any random thing to bully people about. Worst-case scenario is that slowly but unknowingly, you are also damaging your future self, because you are not using your energy properly or your time wisely.

And someday those people you are attempting to hurt may be in positions of power, and have power over you. You may go for a job interview in a company you're dying to work at, only to find that the boss conducting the interview is one of the people you used to make fun of. Or one of your victims may confront you years from now in front of everyone. It's called payback, it's called karma, and right now it's on a nonstop train headed directly to your door.

Instead of bullying, and judging everybody, why don't you join the rest of us in celebrating how unique all of us are? Let's celebrate our gender, our race, our ethnicity, our religion, our appearance, and all the other beautiful differences we hold. Let's do this instead of devouring one another.

Judging someone doesn't define who they are. Striving to give someone pain is what really judges you. Making friends over pathetic "banter" or for a "laugh" shouldn't ever happen. Don't treat others like a joke. If your friends actually laugh because of the stupid jokes you make about others, doesn't it mean that you are the actual clown around here? Accept what is coming your way, or change and improve yourself before there is no turning back.

To the bullied and those with low self-esteem:

"Those who fly solo
often have the strongest wings."

~ Aaron Sledge

Fun fact: bullies can look like ordinary people, like anyone at all. They could even look like a nerd. They could be someone completely unexpected, like the friends you have now.

Now, if you are undergoing physical bullying, don't even think of hiding. It's not the solution, and it will never be. You must seek help from an adult who has high authority as soon as possible—that is, your parents. Once you do, it will be dealt with immediately.

I know so many young kids, especially aged nine to twelve, who have been shoved into a wall or beaten up at school, who have never even thought of telling their parents. Most of them just wait until their parents notice a black eye. If your parents find out, not from you but through another source, it will be too late to handle the situation. And in most cases, the person you are getting bullied by will manage to get away with everything, even when they shouldn't.

But today I want to focus more on the kind of bullying that isn't obvious at all, an issue I call "discrete bullying"—the small, habitual, and constant actions that are purposely done to target, seek harm, and intimidate those who appear more vulnerable than others. This type of bullying happens over a period of time, and can build to something that is as severe as being badly beaten up several times. You must notice whether your friends are the ones maltreating you this way. Notice the way they behave, mainly the way they joke with you. They can be cunning enough to make a joke, purposely targeting you, but then cover it up with a smile.

You Are Not Alone

As we get further into this topic, I would like to make one thing clear. You are not alone even if it may seem like it. You might be afraid of losing your friends, and of course, it's much worse if they were the ones who promised to stay for infinity and beyond. Most of all, you may be terrified to face your bully on a daily basis.

The pain is spread across the whole wide world, and people of different ages undergo a lot worse situations than you do. Who knows? Others might not be as strong or as capable as you are when overcoming and handling issues. We have all gone through this, and we feel for you.

But instead of concentrating on this, I want you to *celebrate*. Celebrate your *own* uniqueness. Celebrate what makes you who you are. But most importantly, accept yourself and *own* your worth. Embrace your appearance and the body you proudly live in during this lifetime. Free from the chains of other people's opinions that have set you back and stopped you from loving yourself. I want you to be empowered enough to understand that you are in fact better off doing what you love and saying what you feel without ever feeling picked on or neglected by society just because you aren't able to align with some insecure peers' misconceptions.

The reason why you stand out might be because you were literally born to stand out. Learn how to accept and appreciate that element of yourself. The more you avoid that, the longer it will take for you to reach your happiness. If you think about it, isn't blending in kind of boring? If everyone were the same, the world would be pretty dull. Being unique spices up your life so much more. This is what makes you more special than others, which is a compliment worth receiving. It's the core of your being.

A lot of people would do anything to stand out and seem different, so if you're being bullied for being different, be thankful that you stand out without having to fight for it. You are beautiful just the way you are, and therefore, you shine. You shine when others can't, and people notice that about you. This is why people target you. It's both good and bad, but it mainly depends on *you* and how you see it, especially what you want the outcome to be. Decide to hold your chin up high instead of drowning in loneliness. Use your loneliness as an advantage.

You need to immediately stop any negative thinking. The isolation you are going through is a beneficial thing because progress requires separation and isolation.

This is exactly what makes you more successful than others. It's what makes you so much ahead of the game. Even though you may not see this right now, let me tell you one thing. A successful person's career starts when they are often left alone, because from that, they have more time to themselves to realize how much potential they hold, and this is what triggers them into succeeding in their own way, in their own space and time.

There will be people cruel enough to make it feel like you will never succeed. Some will even bully the crap out of you and be sly enough to threaten you to keep your mouth shut even when you are willing to raise your voice about it. Instead, stand up for yourself. If you would stand up for a friend while they were getting bullied, then you can do the same for yourself. The bad guys need more people on their side just to go against you. This shows who the real stronger person is. Stand strong and defend yourself as you would defend a friend.

As long as your opinion of yourself remains safe and unaffected, then the pile of crap they throw at you shouldn't affect you at all. Their opinions shouldn't define who you are. They aren't worthy enough for you to change yourself. Only you know your true self, and if you are happy the way you are, it's your job not to let other people's judgments of you ruin your judgment of yourself. You are you, and you best should love and embrace that about yourself. The happier and the more unaffected you remain, the angrier they will become, which will make them gossip even more about you. But this won't affect you if you are your own top priority.

If you become what they want you to become, all sad and gloomy, you have failed, because you have let them achieve their purpose. In order to prevent that, kill them with kindness, and bury them with a smile. Talk to them, not as a friend, but as something neutral, even if you desire to destroy every single shred of happiness they have. Try to not show it, because you must never turn into the villain you are trying to slay. Instead, choose to respond to evil with good.

However, there is a huge difference between standing up for yourself and retaliation. Retaliating and giving them the energy they have given you will make you become more like them. Don't waste your energy or words by aggressively throwing a punch or fighting them verbally. This will only provoke them to hate on you even more. It will never stop if you show them that you care.

You were always seen as a freak right? If they call you out, calmly respond to them in a neutral and cool-headed way. Doing so will leave them dry, with nothing to say. That will reverse this narrative and expose their problem rather than yours because this time, they will be the freaks since they will seem overdramatic and insecure. All this will show how little you care about their existence. You're going to have to show them that you're unbothered. This will make them feel foolish for putting so much energy into tearing you apart.

Plus, don't you think that the only reason why they are talking bad behind your back in the first place is because they are literally behind you? If they are constantly attempting to set you back, yet you still succeed in what you do best, that is the best thing you can do while they are only stuck doing the worst thing. Most importantly, you are the one who is making it this far in life.

I know, it sounds tough and tiring, but you must not give up fighting for your worth. It will be tough at the beginning, but trust me, your final destination is worth the journey. At least you are *still* succeeding after everything, because in reality, they are the ones setting themselves back.

Everything happens for a reason. Everything is the start of something new. You can't control what happens next. The only thing you can control is the outcome of all this. Maybe the purpose of you getting bullied is so they can help motivate you to get to where you want to go in life. Those who bullied you will probably never be as successful as you will be. In the end, this is the consequence that they themselves will have to bear alone. So, take advantage of the control you have.

At least you get to experience things that nobody else gets to, because they aren't *you*. Recognize how lucky YOU are today, to still be able to experience all of this. Even if it's not the best of all the things you want to experience, you are still alive and well. You are lucky because your path is constantly opening ahead of you. You must never stop living your life, and you cannot put the things you love on hold just because a speck of dust is standing on your path to success. Those people aren't important, and you don't want to give them the impression that they are.

Letting Things Slide Won't Help

If they do start to have real feelings and apologize for what they have done to you, just know that this change is not from taking your feelings into consideration. They got into trouble, and they only care about getting out. Don't give them an escape ticket and decide that now you can trust them, and they can be your friend. Steer clear. They have proven that they are betrayers. They must live with the consequences of their bad actions, if they are to grow and to learn. Don't try to shield them from those consequences. Forgive them, but keep them out of your life.

If you choose not to forgive, you won't grow. You will stay stuck in the past. You must forgive the past and learn how to forgive the wrongdoing of others, accept that it happened, and move on. If you refuse to forgive, you will only hold grudges. You won't be able to progress forward if you are always living in the past. Leave all your grudges behind. Forgive, but continue to walk away. Find peace within yourself, independent of whether the bullies are sorry or not.

Unfortunately, for some reason, people tend to never forget the bad things others have said about them or done to them, no matter how long ago it happened. But isn't it funny how people easily forget compliments they received just a few days ago? A lot of negative things stick with us throughout a lifetime because our brain cannot seem to let go. This is why the bad outweighs the good in terms of memory. It's normal, but try your best to not let this happen to you. Pick yourself up from the ashes that they have left YOU to burn in. People don't deserve to see you at your worst, let alone yourself.

The best option is to forgive. But forgiving and forgetting doesn't mean they won't repeat the same mistakes, so don't give them an excuse to change their mind and treat you like trash yet again. You must never get used to people taking advantage of your vulnerability. Many people confuse forgiveness with vulnerability. If they think you are weak for forgiving them, they'll continue to do what they did previously. Forgive them in your heart, without advertising the fact. Never let people take you for granted. You can't let them assume that you are always there in the corner, just hoping they will change their mind and decide to be nice to you.

Some people will let time go by and then start talking to you. They think that time passing is a form of apology. All I hope is that you aren't that gullible. Show them that breaking you down doesn't come for free. The real cost for them is karma. After seeing you succeed in every way they can't, karma will come back and bite them in the—well, you know...

Right now you really can't prove that people were wrong about you. That will only happen when they see who you have become in the future. Use this fact as motivation. Only your future self will define who you are. So make sure that the person you are right now is evolving toward the powerful person the haters doubted you could ever become.

And finally, embrace your flaws, as they are what tells your story and how you far have come on your own. And if you embrace your flaws, you can spread your wings and flourish. After all, haters are our motivators. And honestly, if they constantly watch every move you make, aren't they kind of a fan? Just like celebrities, you have haters because you are special and good at something.

Someone once said, "Don't spend more than five minutes if it's not going to matter in five years." Thank God for protecting you from what you thought you wanted and blessing you with what you didn't know you needed and deserved. If you discover every inch of yourself, and if you have *found* yourself, you have won.

Chapter Four: The Reality Behind Relationships

"Are you naked because he loves you,
or does he love you because you're naked?"

I can see your eyes beam and gleam as you arrive at this delightful chapter. As everyone knows, romantic relationships are one of the biggest, most entertaining, and most challenging aspects of life. Even adults can't seem to master them completely.

Before we start, what do you think of relationships? Being in a great romantic relationship is everyone's dream, isn't it? Most teens love the idea of dating at this age. Mainly between thirteen and sixteen is when my peeps start making their initial move on the road of love, attempting to achieve the teenage dream of marrying their "high school sweetheart"—which hopefully will lead to a successful marriage and, one day, children.

Love is so vital to our well-being. How wonderful would it be to spend the rest of your life with your best friend until you grow old and grey, getting that happy ending you have always wanted? But of course, it's obviously not that simple, even though we would all like it to be. I wouldn't say it's complicated, but we all know there are loads more to it than the classic "happily ever after."

Without even realizing, most teens are desperate to achieve the perfect relationship in a short span of time, which causes them to end up putting their other priorities last. Many get into the wrong relationship with the wrong person, never experiencing the real kind of relationship they truly deserve. This is because they have never been in the *right* relationship with the *right* person.

This *lovely* chapter (no pun intended) will offer advice for teens who find it hard to manage their love life or to deal with the aftermath of a failed relationship. It will also offer lots of suggestions for teens who are in a long-term relationship. If that's working out for you, bravo. Carry on with what you're doing, but listen in all the same, because most of us have blind spots where relationships are concerned, and the wiser you are in this area, the less likely your love life will be to go astray.

I am just here to speak facts and to share the various and great experiences of many people combined. At the same time, don't let my perspectives completely influence yours. Honor your own experience and opinions, but have an open mind.

To the single:

"Far too many people are looking for the right person, instead of trying to be the right person."

~ Gloria Steinem

If you are reading this single, you aren't alone, and I can assure you that finding the right guy or gal should be the last worry on your life list right now. Let up on yourself a little. There's a lot more to live for than having a relationship at an early age. How lucky you are to have this time to yourself, if you use it wisely. You can work on building your character, learning new things, and getting your life together.

But though I say that you should be proud of being single, I'm not suggesting you forget about dating and plan to stay single *forever*. All I am saying is, *live* in the moment. Enjoy the process.

If you are single and sad, look at the positive side of it all. At least your future spouse is taking the time to grow right now, and so are you. Both of you are transforming into the best people you can be, perfecting yourselves for each other when the time comes. By then, both of you will be at your peak. If you both don't take this time to grow right now, meeting each other might never happen, or you might meet but blow it, not recognizing that other person as the right match for you. You may be alone right now, but come on, at least you're not having to struggle with heartbreak and self-doubt. Relationships require a lot of emotion, time, and effort—and especially sacrifices that you may not be willing to make for anyone at this particular moment.

What People Tend to Ignore

Everyone wants that *one* special someone to share love with, someone to be passionate about. Someone worth giving our *all* for—an investment of your time and commitment. Someone who will encourage us to grow and improve, while we inspire them in the same way. Someone whose goals we share and whose interests and work we can get excited about. Most importantly, we want to find someone who is willing to sacrifice for us, and who is worth our sacrificing for.

But did the word "commitment" scare you a little? It's common, but are you worried that you won't be able to give as much as you take? If you have any sort of trepidation about the consequences of relationships, let's do a mini-exercise. All of the questions below are about things that you are 100% ready or not ready to do. Check the boxes of the things you are certain you are capable of doing. Do it in pencil, so if you change your mind or later on achieve that particular thing, then you can change your answer. It's not a test, and it's not for me to see and be impressed by, so check the boxes with full honesty. Don't answer in a hurry. Take some time to contemplate your answers.

	YES	NO
Are you ready to commit?		
Are you ready to be selfless?		
Are you ready to sacrifice your time and effort for someone else?		
Are you ready to support and help the other person grow?		
Are you ready to share your life with someone?		

Answering those questions will help you understand where you truly stand right now regarding relationships.

Imagine that you are hanging out with a good friend and their partner: a wonderful pair. You sit back and watch them hug, kiss, hold hands, and so on. Then they post pictures of themselves together, and you think to yourself, "Well, that's kind of cute," wishing you could do the same. If only you had a partner…

Some people will be rude enough to call you the "third wheel"—the single person who awkwardly hangs out with couples. But hey, note this. The speed that the taken people are moving at is completely different from yours. Those who are taken might think they are better than you, but being single is just as great or even better than being in a relationship right now.

Your "taken" friends may be on the road to heartbreak and self-doubt, while you are in the process of getting to know yourself more and becoming stronger and better. The more mature you are when you do engage in a relationship, the better chance you'll have of surviving it with your spirit intact. Relationships make us vulnerable, so the more self-integrated we are, the more likely we'll be to manage love successfully. The "taken" friends who you envy right now may not be so lucky.

Fun fact: it's usually the single friend who is better at giving relationship advice and helping us with problems in general, because they've grown to be more observant. They take time to self-reflect and think for themselves, which eventually leads to them becoming wiser and more mindful. This is what makes them better at coming up with solutions because they aren't blinded by love, and their judgments and perceptions of reality aren't clouded by their emotions.

For others, for friends who are couples, this isn't always the case. This is why you should pay close attention to how your friends have changed after being taken. Make sure they aren't turning into someone negatively unrecognizable. Distinguish who will be fake enough to ditch the friend for the boyfriend or girlfriend. Those who are like this will constantly make you feel more alone, whether intentionally or unintentionally.

As time goes by, this can start to have a long-term effect on you, since you are constantly being reminded of how single you are. This could trigger you into wanting to be in a relationship even more, making you wonder "Oh, come on. When is it *my* turn?" You might not know this, but the more you think like that, the more you become obsessed with having to "find somebody." That desperate attitude can catapult you into the wrong relationship, because your need to have "what everyone else has," has blinded you.

Don't go getting desperate and needy. Just take it slow, so that when the right relationship comes along, it will last. People so often jump into this or that meaningless, short-term relationship, with this or that person. All of that hustle, just because they are ashamed of being single and are desperate for the feeling of being loved and accepted. And once one relationship ends, the cycle repeats. They patrol to find another, and when things go south yet again, they find themselves doubting their lovability and self-worth.

If you are that person, let's get real. Did you love and accept yourself enough in the first place? If you did, you should have been wise and independent enough to know what you truly need in a partner, instead of reaching for short-term things that you "want." You need to set your mind straight. You might have reached the right age to have a relationship, but the obvious question is, are you *mentally* old enough? Mental age is what really defines you.

This is why modern-day teens get into relationships at a much younger age and at a faster rate than previous generations. It's all because we have the "excuse" that this generation is supposedly "more mature," even when that's not completely the case. That bold statement only makes people believe that they can get away with anything at all. Yes, of course they can, but they eventually fail miserably.

An example of this is short-term relationships. If you have only been in short-term relationships, then you obviously weren't ready enough at the start. All of the months or weeks you spent with your exes should actually add up to how much you should really be spending with one person only. You aren't secure enough to be in a relationship, and this is why you might constantly be on the run from one person to another, which only results in you constantly being left in the ditch, single yet again.

This comes down to the ultimate reason why it's so important to save your time and effort for someone actually worth your while. It's all fun and games at the start until it starts dismantling, piece by piece, and you slowly realize that it's not right. To prevent this disaster, there is simply one thing that can save you: prioritization.

Before getting into a serious and committed relationship, it's vital to recognize your essential *needs* before going after your *wants*. I am pretty sure that 50% of single people are happily living their lives, enjoying the moment, exploring new interests, and giving themselves time to truly discover who they are, actually being grateful to be alone right now and getting things done for themselves.

On the other hand, the other 50% are too desperate to receive love, attention, and affection, mistakenly hopping from one inappropriate partner to another. I mean, do you actually *need* to do this at this exact moment? Do you need to be in a relationship for *survival*?

Setting Some Pre-Relationship Boundaries

If you have high standards, you won't settle for anything less. You won't just dive in with any person at all, without taking the time to completely know and understand them inside and out. Sooner or later, if you just dive in, that person probably won't succeed in giving you what you need. And this is exactly what leads to you breaking up in two or three months, because you weren't familiar enough with the person to begin with. And once that short-term relationship ends, you will feel emptier than before, more vulnerable and desperate. Then your heightened self-doubt will prompt you to chase after yet another superficial and unsatisfying relationship.

Of course you want to experience it all, but don't let that thought consume you. Know your limits and remember to keep your guard up. Letting your guard down for someone you like will make you become someone who is easily let down and screwed over. Then, they just won't take true care of you or value you.

Even if your standards are high, remember that there will be someone who will be able to fulfill them. They will be attracted to you on their own terms without you having to lower your standards, just so you can get into any relationship with anyone at all. You want to be in the right one, not *any* one. Being eager for it can easily blind you to who isn't the right one for you. Give yourself time. Let the right relationship come to you instead of chasing the total opposite. The more you change for the wrong person, the more wrong things you will receive in return.

Now, I don't want to sound like a parent right now. But honesty is the best policy, so I'm just laying it straight out on the table. The fact is, you don't *have to be* in a relationship right now. Let me help elaborate.

Look at yourself. Since we are still young and full of life, what is the huge rush and hustle for? You have so many other worries on your plate right now, so put all your focus on that and take care of those other priorities at this specific moment. This includes your self-growth, spending time with your family, getting to know someone you are interested in, taking care of your studies, starting your career, and reflecting on your future. Such things are the first and foremost priorities that require more of your time and dedication. They must be achieved before achieving other things.

Once you have prioritized these important things, relationships can come after that. So take this time to do what you need to do to get your life up and running. Do what you need to do to *survive* first. There is no such thing as rush, and there shouldn't be, since relationships can happen any time. However, everything else is happening in the "now." You must maintain stability in the things that benefit you *right now*.

When do you think is your ideal or "right" age for marriage? Between twenty and thirty or a bit later, right? Let's assume somewhere in between. I'm not brainy at math, but let's work this out together.

Let's take me as an example. I have about two years left until I graduate high school. By then, I will be around eighteen. After that, I'll have a good four more years until I finish my university degree. By then, I will be at least twenty-one. I see a ton of busy years ahead of me. If I were currently in a relationship, we would have to date for a long time in order to get legally married. Until then, I would have so many other things I need to accomplish, and a relationship would be a distraction.

It can also be extremely frustrating for a couple to be in love and unable to marry because they have to finish their education first. The stress of that can destroy a relationship. I'd rather take the next several years to do everything I need to get done, then date when I'm truly ready and when the time is right. Alternatively, I could focus on one person, forgetting about the other things that need my attention. Or I could focus on those things and not give the relationship the attention it requires to thrive, thereby possibly losing the love of my life.

Well, I'd rather meet Mr. Right up the road, when I'm ready to give a relationship the nurturing it requires, and meanwhile take care of my other priorities, so when the time comes, I'm free and able to be a great partner.

If you are busy handling relationships, you might not be able to achieve the other vital things first, since you are so occupied with the relationship. Focus on yourself, and act on your own terms and conditions, in your own time and way. *Make yourself the priority right now.* Even if you think you are ready to take on a relationship, if you're easily distracted, there is a high chance you won't be able to manage, multitask, or even balance the scales. If you currently can't master your priorities and achieve your goals at the moment, you won't be able to master or even invest the huge amount of time, effort, and emotions into a relationship, either.

Instead, spend this time focusing on being the best person you can be. Once you become that and have achieved the goals you need to accomplish, love and marriage will enter your life at the right time, and you'll be able to give them the attention they deserve.

Another vital thing to remember is that when you are thinking about dating someone or once you are dating them, you must tell your parents and be honest with them about your love life. Earn their support for your dating. That way they can be there in your corner to guide you and give you the best advice along the way. Don't forget: your parents have gone through this, to marriage and beyond. They know what is best for you, especially since they know how to deal with various outcomes in different situations.

If you do decide to date now, observe the person you are interested in. You need to know exactly what you are getting yourself into. Most of all, observe how they stand and deal with things. If they can't deal with things right now, even when not in a relationship, how will they deal with things when they are?

To sum up the points I've been making, single people already tend to know what they want and need, and they won't waste time and effort on the things that currently don't matter. They know that they have all the time in the world to get into a relationship after successfully achieving their current goals. They have a vision, and they are busy building their own well-developed future. They don't rush into relationships because they know that there's time in life for everything.

To the taken:

"A relationship is like a house.
When a lightbulb burns out,
you do not go and find another house;
you fix the lightbulb."

~ Laura Gibson

The Question of Sex

The following few paragraphs are directed mainly to older teens. Know that you are in total control of your body, your decisions, your actions, and the speed your relationship is moving at. You are capable of doing whatever floats your boat, since no one can stop you or control the decisions you make, but yourself. But note that you face some serious consequences when you make choices that are actually bad for you.

If sex was you and your partner's decision, that's one thing. But if they are forcing and manipulating you into doing things you don't want to do, saying, "If you loved me, you would do it," or "If you don't do it, I'll leave you," it's never too late to dump their ass. Save yourself. You deserve way better. Don't even think of saying, "We already made it so far and we have been dating for ages, so okay, it's fine. I'll do it." Bit delusional, huh?

Get rid of them. Don't let the fact that you dated for ages be an excuse to carry on and obey them, especially when deep down you know it's not right. Don't get desperate and think they will forever be the only source of love and affection for you. You need to think for yourself and distinguish what is right from wrong. If you are sensible enough, you will be able to value and love yourself for what is within you, to know what you truly deserve, and just simply walk away. You *have* got boundaries, right? Well, then use them.

You should know that sort of selfish, manipulative person doesn't deserve you. Wake up and realize that if they truly loved you, they wouldn't pressure you into anything because they would respect your decisions. Their behavior underscores what it really is that attracts them to you. It isn't the person inside. It's your body. They value their selfish lust over what is good for you. A person like this will never make you happy, because they don't care about you, despite their fine words to the contrary. Up the road, they will cheat and leave you, perhaps with several children in tow, because pleasure is their top priority. Don't let such a jerk ruin your life.

If you aren't stupid, you will know that you must never be forced or pressured to give up your body for free just for someone you "love" (or so you think) just to please them by doing things you aren't comfortable with. An ideal partner (someone you deserve) would take as much time as possible to progress with you, bit by bit. Not rip your clothes off and treat you like a one-night stand just for the sake of their own pleasure. As someone said, "Don't let people treat you like a cigarette. They only use you when they're bored and step on you when they're done."

Now we can involve the minors. So, what can we certainly learn from this, kids? Now we know that the love the other person gives you should never define your worth. Their love only exists to help, uplift, and nurture you, not to make you feel *valued* all of a sudden. Unfortunately, I can't make dramatic pauses when I'm writing, but take a wild guess as to which source of love is the *most* important. Drum roll... self-love! It's one of the most valuable things in life. Lack that, and you lack everything. If you are in a relationship, and you lack self-love, your partner will be burdened and have to overextend themselves just because you couldn't love yourself in the first place. No one can give more than they should. It's impossible. It's tiring and exhausting.

You must put love into yourself before putting it into others. This is why if you lack self-love, it's a dead-end for you. This is what people mean when they say, "You can't love someone without loving yourself." This is why you must never, *ever*, get together with someone who is insecure. You will just end up hating yourself. They will constantly ask you who you are texting, check your phone when you aren't there, ask where you're going and who you are meeting up with, and always tell you that you deserve someone better. They will constantly remind you how bad they are at something, tell you how much they hate themselves, and list things about themselves they wish could be changed.

I mean, if they don't see any good in themselves, how can they expect you to? And then there is you—the secure person who is always pampering them, saying "Hey, no, you aren't like that. You are so good at what you do. You are beautiful just the way you are. I love you, don't say that." Stop clowning. If you are always saying that and reminding them of their worth, how emotionally exhausting will it be?

And I tell you, if they say, "You deserve someone better" (which often happens when they are being sensitive and emotional), listen to what they are truly saying. It's a sign of how insecure they really are. And since insecure people are known to be vulnerable, they mean it. Plus, you really do deserve much better, especially if they keep on ruining your day by saying things like that. A lot of negativity will be brought into your once-upon-a-time peaceful life, until you won't be immune to it anymore. You'll start to grow negative yourself. This kind of relationship is a curse.

Standards versus Expectations

Another thing we must learn is the importance of maintaining high standards. Doing so will help you get an idea of what you truly deserve. This can also help you see whether you are being treated properly and respected highly in your relationship, or not. If you don't have high standards, then don't expect anything great, because if you get treated like trash repeatedly, you won't even notice it.

Even though it's good to have high standards, remember that standards and expectations are two different things. Standards are a level of quality of something or someone, but expectations are what you expect to get from the other person, and specific things you expect them to do for you. In relationships, both sides have different expectations of what should be coming from the other.

It's great to have high standards, but not unreasonable or selfish expectations. Just because you expect a lot from someone doesn't mean they're going to deliver. Maybe they don't want to, or maybe they're just unable to. If your expectations are unreasonable or too self-centered, the other person won't be able to fulfill them all. Then you'll start doubting whether they're good enough, whether you love them, whether they're making the effort, and so forth, when the real problem is you.

Please don't overthink and don't rush their ability. They must move at their own pace. Don't rush them to be romantic for your own sake. If they're going to be romantic, they shouldn't be doing it only for you—they should also be doing it on behalf of themselves. If you're forcing them to do stuff for you, then what you're getting isn't worth receiving, because it doesn't come from a place of genuineness. Such behavior is nothing but controlling and selfish. The other person must constantly strive to prove themselves to you, and that is exhausting.

Your job in a relationship is to make sure the flame is still burning even when enduring a storm. Make it last long, which translates to "dating to marry." Not being extreme here, but a relationship is basically a marriage, but without the ring. It's a commitment. It's unity. You were designed and built as a team to take on the world together. To fight and conquer one at a time, to help each other grow and improve, to be a fan of each other, to invest time, and so on.

If marriage is not in the picture, then why are you in a relationship with them? Is there a point in dating them? Even if the thought of marriage has never occurred to you, then I am still talking about long-term relationships, meaning years—not short, pathetic, and flimsy months here and there to keep you entertained. You shouldn't be playing around and tragically entertaining yourself out of your lonesomeness. Not to be harsh, but you will end up broken if you play around like that. This is why dating to marry is *vital*. You must practice how to commit to one person only. This prevents you from wasting time on other people who are completely unworthy of your time.

If you don't see you and your partner reaching endgame, or if the word "years" actually sounds like centuries to your ears, then that clearly means you just don't have the vision or drive to make "dating to marry" possible, or the timing just isn't right. Timing is key, but time won't always be on your side. You need everything to be placed in the right spot and at the right time for things to work out well. Take it slow so you won't screw the timing up. And make the wisest decisions on which direction the relationship is heading, without rush. At the same time, don't let the relationship control you. You control the relationship.

"Control" means that you must take full responsibility for any disputes or problems that happen between you. Whatever the problem, you need to maintain a single person's mentality when solving it, since single people aren't blinded by love. Don't let your real emotions get in the way of accepting reality. Don't blame other people for problems between you and your partner. That only makes things messier. This happens when one person in the couple can't face the reality that something could be their fault.

Blaming others can't possibly fix things between you and your partner. The responsibility is still there and you can never run away from it, so don't pretend that it's okay to spread it around to other people who shouldn't be involved. It's your job to admit, accept, and *bear* responsibility.

That being said, there will be people who will step in and try to destroy your relationship. In that case, they want to selfishly steal either you or your partner because they envy what you guys have. So, you better show them it ain't easy to get it for free.

Most of all, don't give in to temptation. You could, but is it really worth letting it all go? Your relationship shouldn't be easy for others to break apart, but strong enough to withstand storms and external threats. The reason why you are together in the first place is because you basically made a deal to never let outside negative influences intertwine with the way you operate as a team. Know your place, and most importantly, don't abuse it.

If you notice that your relationship is in the crosshairs of other people's malicious intentions, you could give them the attention they want and call them out for it. Or, you could let your partner know, and both of you can discuss the matter privately, tackling the problem together on your own terms.

Of course, the second option is the wisest to go with. The whole point of stealing the spark that exists between you and your partner is so they can get your attention. Once they do, there is a risk of you and your partner not being able to give enough attention to each other, you get distant, then *boom*, you break up, then the brat steals the weakened partner, leaving you with zilch.

During difficult situations, it's your job to recognize what is going on, especially without letting problems slide. You must stand up for each other and overcome things that people never thought you could. You are the strong couple that can go through hell and back to survive, right? Well, prove it, and do it as many times as you need to until you defeat what comes your way.

If things get carried too far and if you have any disputes, remember that it's you and your significant other versus the problem, *not* you versus him or her. I mean, they are called your "partner" for a reason.

Moving on to problems between the partners themselves, one of the biggest problems that arise is second thoughts, which is usually your intuition signaling to you that something isn't right. If you're having doubts about your partner, it may be because you've developed trust issues over time because they have given you a reason to doubt their loyalty or sincerity, making you insecure in the relationship. It's something that can eat away at almost everything.

To prevent this, fully open up to them about your concerns. When you do, don't go all crazy FBI and don't make careless assumptions without any proof. Because if you do, it will just be a one-sided affliction caused by something that may not exist. Just ask them nicely. Make sure your wording is correct because you don't want any misunderstandings between the two of you. Get straight to the point as to what has been troubling you, because not doing so can lead to you having the same conversation repeatedly.

The Danger of Secrecy

Of course, you can also ask others for advice. But note that anyone you open up to about your relationship can be snitches at any point (which you must be cautious about). They might know a side of your relationship that others may not, meaning they have more of a risk of easily spreading private information about your relationship.

This can damage your relationship if there's something your partner might not have wanted anyone else to know. Once you ruin your partner's trust in you, it's like shattered glass. Apologizing after it's been destroyed won't change a thing. It won't go back to being the same. The relationship will forever remain broken. Never abuse the trust you worked so hard to gain.

Secrecy abuses trust as well. It's good to have privacy in the relationship, but there is a difference between protecting the relationship's private matters from others, and hiding you and the relationship from other people. Some people will have the audacity to ask you to "take it underground," which is highly unacceptable. They are just ashamed of you. They aren't proud to be with you, which is part of the point of being in a relationship.

If they were actually proud to have you, they would happily tell others and display it to the whole world, saying, "Hey look, he/she is mine." But if they are keeping you buried and at bay from the public and if they lie to their family about you, do the right thing and confront them about it. If they refuse to listen or have no solution to this problem, be strong enough to walk away. Why? Because as I have said before, you must never settle for anything less than what you deserve.

Your partner and you should be willing to make sacrifices for each other and for the relationship. You both must put in the effort if you want this to survive. If either of you give up on the other for no good reason, shame on you. If that happens, all you have done all these months or years is waste your time.

This is why couples who have dated for many years deserve a lot of admiration and respect. They manage to successfully graduate high school together, maybe attend separate universities, yet still find a way to reunite after it all. They even end up getting married and having children of their own. Outsiders say, "That seems pretty easy," without knowing the difficulties involved. Not many people are as strong as such couples, getting that far in life, while prioritizing everything else behind the scenes.

They have fought for a lot and were willing to sacrifice a lot just to be together. In the end, the reward for all their efforts was actually ending up together. How great is that? But remember, just because it's your plan to get married to your high-school love, don't assume your partner feels the same way.

The pressure against ending up together a decade later is intense. Only time will tell, and if it's meant to be, it will be. If something happens that causes the two of you to take separate paths, such as attending different schools or living in different towns on account of a job, this doesn't mean you need to end things completely. The process just requires more trust and independence, hopefully nothing more than that. Long-distance relationships are unpredictable because what happens next is unpredictable. Don't force things. You can easily be let down if things don't go your way. This is why it's best to let things flow. If you support each other's best interests, you will come back together in the end if it's meant to be.

If you end up in different states or countries for school, or work in a different city from each other, it still may all work out. If you have an outstanding offer for a school or career position that requires you to live in a different place than your partner, you shouldn't turn that down just for them. There are so many new opportunities that lie ahead of you. Never stop chasing them for someone you love, because in time you would come to resent them for that. And if you end up dumping your dreams just for them, remember they could easily dump you, too. If you give up on your dreams for your partner, you will forever regret not making the right decision for yourself. I mean, there is a higher chance of the person dumping you than of the offer itself dumping you. Think wisely, and take the smart route.

When you get an offer, you will obviously need to find a way to break it to them. Remember to do it face-to-face and tell them in a calm and comforting tone. The reason why you must do it face-to-face instead of over the phone is because it's just more respectful and caring. Plus, you can pay close attention to their reaction and their facial expressions, because you want to know their true feelings on the matter.

Of course, it will take time for them to digest the news, so allow them for that. In the end, if they optimistically and enthusiastically encourage you to go for it, then they do indeed respect and support your life choices. This shows how much they are willing to work through long-distance no matter what.

The same goes if your partner gets an offer that requires them to move away from *you*. What's best for them and their goals should be your priority, not keeping them by your side in the same town. These are the years when the decisions you make about education and career will affect the outcome of the rest of your lives. If you walk away from educational or career opportunities during the years when those should be your priority, in the long run, you're cheating not only yourself but your future self. So it isn't selfish to put these things first. Allow your partner to move away if they need to, and allow yourself to do the same. Distance won't destroy the relationship if you're meant to be together. Prioritize correctly, and it will all work out in the end.

If you have been multitasking your relationship and your priorities all along, then you are strong enough to do it again, but at a distance. It's just distance. It's intangible. It's only a few miles between you, and honestly, it shouldn't mean anything when someone means everything to you.

There is still communication—which is key to sustaining a long-distance relationship, of course. After all, you are at an advantage because you have social media. The older generations didn't have that, yet they managed better than those of us who do have it. So you are going to have to make time to communicate with your partner on a day-to-day basis. Whether it's a short or long conversation, keep the momentum going.

Call each other and tell one another how your day went. If you can't call them due to busyness, at least give them a solid reason instead of ghosting them for hours or days. That is how a relationship survives long-term. It's as simple as this. Lack of communication just contributes to you assuming rather than knowing how the other person is doing, which only leads to doubt and jumping to conclusions. This is why assumption is the lowest form of knowledge.

But let's rewind for a second. What if you get an excellent offer, and rather than being happy for you, they want you not to take it? Try to talk it out and negotiate a plan that will make them feel comfortable and hopeful about the future of your relationship, in spite of you being away. In the end, they will need to respect your decision and go with it, but do what you can to meet them halfway.

If they are resentful about it though, there's a high chance they will cheat once you are gone, or will decide to dump you because they've met someone else. If they refuse to support you, keep on thinking big and do what is best for you anyway. Make your dreams your top priority. If they won't take part in making it happen, kiss them goodbye. If they don't prioritize your priorities, they don't prioritize you as a person. They don't truly have your best welfare at heart, and the relationship will end soon, whether you are the one to do it or you wait for them to do it down the road.

*"Never chase love, affection, or attention.
If it isn't given freely by another person,
it isn't worth having."*

~ Ashley Purdy

Qualities of an Ideal Partner

Last but not least, let me give you my list of traits of a good partner. None of us always measure up, but we should strive for these ideals. Be grateful if you find a partner who embodies *most of* them.

Partners should always:

1. **Trust one another**. Trust is one of the most important things a partner must be able to provide. Both of you must let each other go out into the world, but trust that you will return without a scratch. This links to loyalty.

2. **Be honest**. Both of you must be willing to share things open-heartedly, instead of hiding things from each other. You must be willing to honestly negotiate and communicate about personal issues and misunderstandings. Honesty builds security and trust.

3. **Be positive**—a real requirement. You need someone who looks for the good in every situation. Even when things go south, they should be a "glass half-full, not half-empty" sort of person. Being in love with an optimistic person can change your perspective on life even if you yourself may not be the most positive person in the world. Positivity conquers negativity, and you guys need it for the relationship to survive. Positivity is super important for the mental health of you both. It's how you empower each other.

4. **Know they can always say no** to something they don't want to do, and that their partner will respect their decision.

5. **Listen attentively** to the other and accept everything about the other—their problems, their secrets, and their flaws included.

6. **Be supportive** of the other's decisions, and help and uplift them along the way. Embrace each other's past and present, and encourage each other's future.

7. **Be themselves** around their partner, because they wouldn't want their partner loving them for something they're not.

8. **Be giving and ready to commit**. If one person receives more than the other, it's unfair. The output of the relationship heavily depends on the input. They must treat their partner as a top priority, but also maintain their own space, respect their partner's space, and allow themselves and their partner time to grow.

9. **Be flexible and open to good changes**. Work on self-improvement and be willing to make improvements that are needed within the relationship.

10. **Take responsibility** for their own words and actions. Apologize when they know a mistake is their own doing instead of putting blame on other people.

11. **Be respectful and well-mannered**, never taking their partner for granted. Respect the other's schedule and their friends, even if you may not like them as much.

12. **Defend and protect their partner** at all times from other people's bad intentions or when someone is mistreating their partner.

Partners should never:

1. **Cheat—** a big no, a huge turnoff. If you are small enough to cheat on someone who has stood by your side through thick and thin, you cheat yourself out of happiness, because you'll never deserve someone's loyalty again.

2. **Lie or keep secrets from their partner.** You may think you're protecting yourself, when in truth, you're doing the opposite.

3. **Make their partner feel insecure or inferior**.

4. **Make empty promises**. This only damages trust. This also shows how little commitment has been put into the relationship.

5. **Be selfish** by being controlling. Let them have freedom, but of course with boundaries. After

all, if they abuse their freedom, at least you did your part.

6. **Rush their partner**. Everyone moves at their own pace, so please accept your partner's.

7. **Change themselves for their partner.** Only change yourself to improve yourself for your own sake, not to satisfy the other person. If that is required of you, they don't love you enough to accept you for who you are.

8. **Mistreat their partner or talk behind their back**.

9. **Argue over petty matters** or unfairly place blame on the partner.

10. **Go MIA after an argument** instead of talking things out. Ignoring the other person's calls or texts is just teaching them how to live without you.

11. **Give up on the relationship** after something small happens.

12. **Give up their dreams** and priorities for the other person.

To the ladies out there:

*"Don't be a woman who needs a man.
Be a woman who a man needs."*

This message is specifically directed to the ladies, but I recommend the gentlemen out there still read this section, as some parts aren't completely confined to the ladies. Or you can read this to better understand what goes on, on the girl's side of a relationship.

Do Yourself a Favor

Let me address something that hasn't been brought to our attention much. It's something that I believe women in general need to improve on.

Back in the day, women had different-sized waists, breasts, and thighs, and that was celebrated. Each feminine figure from coast to coast was diverse in its own beautiful and unique way. Women all lived their lives, not giving a damn for the way they looked, but only feeling comfortable and joyful in the things they did freely.

However, this gradually stopped, as men's intentions shifted and women's perspectives on being validated evolved. The majority of women in today's society believe they are required to become more experienced in bed and to change for other people's liking just to feel loved and accepted by others *and* themselves. I hate to say it, but nowadays most girls are growing up looking the same and believing the same: that the only way to be attractive is to work out tirelessly to achieve the hourglass figure; to make themselves look like everybody else.

How saddening and heart-breaking is this? *Real* women never strive for perfection. They embrace the body they were given because they know that self-love is the real source of validation. You don't need to overextend yourself by doing uncomfortable things just to make a guy fall for you. You mustn't worry about whether your body is good enough for a guy or not. It's unnecessary. This would only happen if you were with the wrong one, because the right guy will never make you feel this way, intentionally or not.

You aren't required to show your body off or use it to seduce or provoke men into liking you. There's no need for that. Don't become someone unrecognizable just to attract some guy. If you do this, you won't only end up losing him, but you'll end up losing yourself, too. When you do, it will be easier for guys to only use you for sex, and no one wants to be played with like that.

There are guys out there who are manipulative enough to do anything to put their stick into a hole just for pleasure. Don't be foolish to let guys take advantage of you just for their own benefit. You are worth more than being toyed around with. If you treat yourself like a sex object, then don't expect others to treat you any better than that. Yet girls are still eager to show off their skin, breasts, and thighs as if they were in KFC. I mean, come on. Even prostitutes don't do it for free. So for your own sake, don't go cheaper than them. If a guy requires that of you, send him to his local brothel instead of you doing the work. At the end of the day, it's all about the class.

If you make him love you for something your body isn't, he will be attracted to something that isn't real, and yes, this may increase your self-esteem for a short while, but in the long-run, it will only make you rely on that fake side of you more than what is *real* about you. Think about it. The only thing you are required to show off is your heart and the great person you are on the inside. Once you are beautiful on the inside, everything else about you becomes beautiful, too, making you stand out from the crowd.

The Man You Truly Deserve

Do yourself a huge favor and own your worth. Stride proudly with confidence. When you do, the right guy will automatically flow to you because you attract realness. Once you attract realness, the other person will return the same or even greater to you. You won't have to chase or pursue a man. The right guy for you will love you for you. But until then, you need to learn how to embrace your flaws. Embrace your body. It's your nature. You should never feel the need to change that. Trust me on this.

When I say that he will love you entirely, this doesn't only include how pretty you may be or how slim you may appear. This also includes your acne, your dehydrated skin, your crooked teeth, your monobrow, your leg hair, your stretch marks, your height, your weight, the dimples on your back, the unique curves your body makes, you name it. If he doesn't love every single piece that completes the puzzle of your body, ditch him, sis. Mr. Right will love every single inch of your body that you are insecure about. Why? Because none of that matters! He will love you for you.

Meanwhile, if you do look hot, and if this is the tool you use to attract horny guys, congrats. We get it, you are eye candy. But if you are willing to date someone based on their looks, just don't date at all. It's a fact that if you pursue someone entirely based on their looks, people will get used to you after a short while, then find you completely boring and unattractive. You can be the hottest woman alive, but if you don't work on what is more important (which is clearly not your looks), then you will come off as ugly.

Instead of working on your appearance glow-up, work on your spiritual glow-up. This is exactly why girls who aren't the prettiest are always the ones who find a true man before the hottest girls do. Why? Because they have the prettiest souls. Even if you look hot, if you can't keep up with his expectations of you and your body, he will completely drop you and seek some other girl. You are worth so much more than this.

Don't let him treat you like some conquest. If you don't show that you are worth so much more than that, many guys will never have the drive to keep you once they have the impression that you are easy to get. When this happens, the guy will completely ignore your boundaries. He will laugh at them, because he knows your boundaries don't hold true.

Instead, you need to be the "one in a million" type of girl. Even when he has you, you need to prove to him that you are worth fighting for. I am sick of girls hanging onto guys who don't even treat them right just because they fear being alone and feeling unwanted. Don't cling to him like a lost puppy, and make sure you aren't treated that way. A woman should never have to chase a man. Doing so is the only way you will ever drop your crown. If he is a real man, he won't go anywhere, and you won't have to do the clinging.

A real man is a chivalrous and well-mannered gentleman, but girls should do their part as well. Even though guys might be expected to pay for everything, at least do or pay for *something*. For example, if he pays for the cinema tickets, you could jump in and pay for the snacks. If he opens the car door for you, you can reach over and unlock his door from the inside before he walks over. You see? It's simple. Your man shouldn't have to do every single thing for you without anything in return. Even though you shouldn't owe a guy anything, you shouldn't get without giving a little, you know? After all, it's all about teamwork.

Last but not least, we women need to rise above becoming fragile and vulnerable by depending on men in the relationship. I am tired of people presuming girls are never powerful partners in relationships. Girls have grown to become much stronger. We have risen to own power in society. You cannot let people's stereotypical judgments define you. If men expect women to be their little minions, they surely don't know that the woman plays a *much* greater role than that in the relationship, marriage, and beyond.

Women are the necks of the head. We direct the man to do greater, and it's usually the guy who transforms himself into a better person just because he was under the good influence of the woman. Be this woman. We women are equally as powerful as men. Some may say even more powerful. Just because they are physically bigger doesn't mean you are inferior or less entitled to have your own say. You are also in total control. And this? This is the power of women.

To the gentlemen out there:

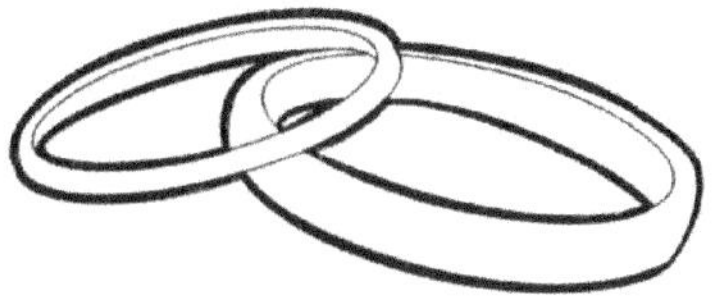

"Would you ever let your daughter marry a man like you?"

~ Samantha de Senna Fernandes

Well, that is a pretty deep and valid question you should consider asking yourself, guys. For now, reflect on the type of man you have grown up to be. The single thought of your future daughter possibly marrying a man like you is quite daunting, isn't it? Unless you are a decent gentleman, in which case there should be no worry at all.

As you know, this message is directed to the men out there, but I recommend the girls read this section also, as some areas may apply to you as well. However, to the guys out there, if some of the things I say here don't apply to you, consider yourselves lucky. I am just directing these words to those who aren't aware of certain things that they should be aware of while in a relationship.

Are You the Real Deal?

It has come to my attention that guys from younger generations tend to be, let's say, boys. Not men. It's an obvious fact that *a lot* of girls out here prefer men over boys. There is a huge difference between the two, not just in physical age, but in emotional age.

When I say "men," I don't mean full-grown men. I am referring to guys who know how to *act* like a grown man—a gentleman, as it were. This consists of a guy who is spiritually, mentally, and physically willing to deal with problems with full responsibility, ensuring that the relationship is moving to a safe *place,* at a safe *pace.* You are her protection and her guard. You are the shield against difficult times, not only hers and yours, but against the obstacles the relationship faces. It's your *job* to make a woman's life easier. The same applies to women when they're in a relationship. Your job, ladies, is to protect your man. This is basically what we sign up for once we step into the spotlight of being "taken."

There is one little secret that I am more than willing to share with you, guys. Hopefully this can help clear up your confusion about why you sometimes get dumped and help you understand women more. I know I personally do this, and I'm pretty sure that 99% of other girls do the same. The other 1% just don't think about it, or they just lack some serious knowledge.

When we girls decide on whether we will date or marry a guy, we clearly know it's not our job to turn a boy into a man. This is because we cannot turn a guy into something he isn't yet ready to be. Plus, it's not a woman's job, and no one can force that change in you. A real man would never depend on anyone to turn him into a man. Your transformation depends on you and only you, but I will let you know one more thing.

Every girl notices whether or not you know how to be a real man in a relationship. If you don't, this is where everything goes south. This thought has definitely slipped into her mind just before she dumps you. Girls look at the overall picture and think deeply about possible outcomes of different situations. And trust me on this: you have no escape once she cracks the code and realizes you are not able to own up and take responsibility. Then she sees you only as someone pathetic. Remember, it isn't smart to doubt her intuition, because most of the time it's right.

This is one of the reasons why girls end things with guys, or just don't date them at all. Of course, it's also a woman's responsibility to make the relationship as stable as possible, too, but I find that it's predominantly important for the guy to set a good example. If guys don't own up to their responsibility in the relationship, then the girl will soon follow.

Don't get me wrong, though. I am not saying that girls *depend* on men to protect them and to solve all of their problems. If a girl has this assumption, then you are with the wrong girl, dude. It's unfair for a woman to expect this, and she needs to take responsibility for solving her own problems. But what she wants is for her man to provide a kind of emotional shield against the difficulties she's facing, through his compassion and willingness to listen.

She doesn't want you to magically fix everything for her. She just wants you to support her as she works through her own challenges. You will have to not only promise, but also *prove* that she won't face the trials of life alone. That way, she will be able to trust you with anything and everything. If a girl feels that this isn't the case, she won't feel secure. If you don't understand this, you may not be having much luck at the boyfriend game. Now, this is what a real man does without any excuse and without even blinking. To be protective is a real man's instinct.

A real man would also never settle for a girl who is desperate and insecure. You can tell that this is the case when her behavior correlates with desperation. Of course, it won't end well. Don't let yourself become the last and the only option that a girl has. When you find a girl who's worth it, try your hardest to chase her and earn her heart. Do so until she sees only *you* even when others try to claim her.

Why Chivalry Matters

You might not be able to fulfill all of your girl's hopes for what a boyfriend should be, but at least try your best. In case you don't know, girls like you to do nice things for them, but they don't want to tell you because they don't want to seem bossy and because they don't want to beg for it. If a chivalrous act is her idea and not yours, it doesn't hold much value. For example, if she has to ask you to surprise her with flowers now and then, or to remember her birthday, the joy goes out of the surprise.

To completely earn her heart, remember that girls *love* small things, meaning cute and romantic gestures. This doesn't mean buying her huge rose bouquets, going on dates every night, or buying her stuffed teddy bears and chocolate every day. That would be expensive and exhausting. Save that stuff for important events, like birthdays and your anniversary.

When I say "small gestures" are appreciated, I literally mean "small." Things like hugs and cuddles, holding hands, sending a loving text or email, or better yet a card, and other types of cute and also chivalrous actions, like opening the door for her and closing it behind her, pulling out her chair at dinner, sitting on the outside when you're in a booth, putting your coat over her shoulders when she's cold, walking on the outside of the sidewalk to ensure she is safe on the inside, away from the street and the cars, showing her off to the public and introducing her to your friends, giving her a bouquet of wildflowers you picked, buying her a favorite candy bar, and so on.

Doing such things will not only show that you care but will help to make her never doubt her protection and safety when in your presence. Even though these are little and fairly simple actions, she will never forget them, and will forever treasure them.

If your girl is always the first to text or to do something affectionate, you aren't holding up your end of the relationship, and she will doubt whether you truly care for her. If you aren't giving in these ways, you don't deserve to receive her affection, because you are not making an effort. Be romantic and make the move, but try not to work excessively out of your comfort zone. Just do what you can, but at the same time, don't be lazy and don't just do it once or twice. You must continue the momentum by doing these actions of affection.

By the way, simple acts of politeness, such as opening doors for girls, should be standard behavior for guys who are single, not just for guys with a girlfriend. Girls find guys more attractive who behave chivalrously.

Flirt with your girl even when you have already captured her heart. Don't just drop the chivalry when you get her, or she'll think you don't really care. You must still be willing to chase her, even if your friends may call you a "simp"—which means "a male who should feel shame in treating a girl properly." Such teasing is unfortunate, because it gives boys the impression that it isn't manly to love wholeheartedly or to respect a woman. Even though it's a joke, it actually promotes sexism. It prevents guys from trying in a relationship because their male peers keep feeding them the imagery of "simp."

Let this not be the case with you. Rise above their foolishness. Love wholeheartedly. It isn't your buddies you need to win, but your girl. If you hold back your affection, hoping to look cool, she'll start to think about finding someone better and more loving. You are you, and it is okay to love. When you are the first to express affection, she will follow suit. She will feel more wanted and much safer and secure with you, and I am 100% sure she will make you feel the same or even greater. The less input there is in the relationship, the less output there will be. So the more, the better.

It's like what William Golding said: "Whatever you give a woman, she will make greater. If you give her sperm, she'll give you a baby. If you give her a house, she'll give you a home. If you give her groceries, she'll give you a meal. If you give her a smile, she'll give you her heart. She multiplies and enlarges what is given to her." What a beautiful statement. Don't abuse and mistreat this.

Toxic Masculinity

If you don't get anything out of doing great things for your girl, then at least you can tell yourself that you have tried your utter best, and if she chooses to let you go, then at least you know it's not because you let her down in this regard. If things don't go your way even when you have given it your all, feel free to express your feelings. If that means crying, go ahead. Just because you are a man doesn't mean you aren't allowed to cry. Those who think otherwise believe in toxic masculinity.

All men cry, and I think it's masculine. Sometimes it's how you feel and you can't change that. Don't let people strip that right away from you. Handle things by acknowledging your feelings, instead of denying them and drowning your sorrows by drinking or becoming a playboy. Playboys are broken boys who only chase girls with the best figure, who objectify women, and are incapable of authenticity and emotional intimacy with anyone. If you intend to flirt with all girls the same way, then how will you settle down and catch real feelings for someone who is unique? How will you actually know who the right one is for you? Now this is real toxic masculinity.

Unfortunately, I myself have had countless encounters with various playboys, but there is one I will never forget. One summer, I got a text from a guy who I had seen but never met. The text said, "Meet me at the park at 3 pm." For some reason, I felt targeted even when it wasn't a big deal. My response to that text was, "I'm sorry. I have a boyfriend," and his reply back was "Ouch." I mean, how wrong was this in many contexts?

One, his behavior and the way he "gets" a girl isn't right as it seems he's just trying to get with anyone. And two, I can't believe that I had to label myself as "taken" even when I wasn't at all. No girl should feel this way. No girl should be scared enough to say they have a boyfriend just because they feel like prey.

"Just because someone stopped loving you, it doesn't mean you should stop loving yourself."

~ Samantha de Senna Fernandes

Breakups and Their Sting

Now I'll be talking to both guys and girls again. Let's talk about when a relationship ends. You might be either the dumper or the dumpee. Either way, everyone knows that both sides suck, since a breakup deeply affects one's emotional and mental health. Once we mention the 'B' word, we all get nostalgic flashbacks of how it felt and especially the face of the person who caused it.

Are you one of those very young teens who tend to break up with a person without a valid reason? Maybe you give phony excuses, like "Oh, the relationship got boring over time, and I just lost feelings for them." Ha ha, okay. Let's be honest, teens just use this as an escape route out of a relationship that turned out to be a mistake. We all know that excuse is not solid enough.

To set things straight, the reason why you lost feelings for them was simply because what you shared wasn't genuine enough. Or perhaps it was just a crush, and you weren't in love for real. If it "got boring" over time, it's probably because you weren't doing any growing with the other person. If you were growing, you would enjoy learning new things together, and new things about the other person. Were you scared of growing with them? If so, that means you aren't ready to commit to someone yet.

It's also important to understand that even in the best of relationships, there will be times that are fun, boring, happy, sad, annoying, deep, bright, and dark. A relationship isn't always a rose garden. Your time spent with your partner will be full of ups and downs. You must never expect a relationship to always be fun. That's a fantasy. Those pictures you see on social media are not real. Everything in the media is created to craft the image they want you to see. Don't fall for it. Only stable couples don't mind spending boring times together, and they don't feel obliged to showcase things online.

Speaking about the social media world, if you want to break up with someone, obviously the right thing to do is to come clean and give them the honest reason, face-to-face, firmly and clearly. Breaking it to them over text or on the phone is childish. Plus, once you do that, it's made crystal clear that you are immature and unable to bear responsibility. The person you're breaking up with has invested their time and emotions in you. The least you can do is have the decency to explain why it didn't work out for you, to their face.

If a person gets broken up with, again and again, and is never told why, they never learn what they are doing wrong, and never have the opportunity to grow and improve themselves. We owe it to one another, as decent human beings, to be honest with our partners when we decide to break up.

Another famous excuse some kids give for breaking up is something along the lines of "I'm breaking up with you because I'm too busy and I need to focus on myself." Huh? I didn't quite catch that. That counts as zero of a reason. Life only gets busier and harder to deal with as we mature, going from teenage years into adulthood. If you are going to keep ending things because you are "busy" every time, then you will never be able to stabilize and settle down in a relationship. I mean, life only gets harder to handle. Don't run. Only end things if the other person proves to be unworthy, or if the relationship is hurting your mental health, because that is a serious priority. Mental health must always come first. But many people use mental health as an excuse, even when their mental health is completely fine.

Heartbroken, Now What?

After breakups happen, people tend to get back together (which I know is something a lot of you are huge fans of). But just note one thing: a break is the beginning of the end. You are putting your relationship at pause, which isn't supposed to happen if your relationship is healthy. If you are considering a break, conditions between you might not return to how it was before, since taking a break is distancing yourself from the other person, which should be the last thing you want to do.

Now we can move on to talking about those who have broken up for real. I don't like saying the word "revenge," but that is the first thing people think of after splitting apart. Don't concentrate on getting revenge against the other broken half. You shouldn't feel you have to prove to your ex that you are better off without them.

Even if you are, it has got nothing to do with them now. You are not in competition with them, nor do you have to hurry and find a new partner before they do. Instead, remember that the best comeback to heartbreak is proving to yourself that you are much better than the person you were *during* the heartbreak. Your "revenge," as it were, is the moment they see you succeed a lot more emotionally and mentally, only to end up rising much higher than the last state you were in.

Honestly, people may see you progress to the point where they feel embarrassed for overestimating your vulnerability when you broke up. All you need to remember this time is that there is someone much better on offer for you in the future. But meanwhile, you should try to remain neutral friends with your ex and stay on good terms with them. Everyone believes in the "you have to hate your ex" thing, but there's no need for that. You should be grown-up enough not to treat them badly by ranting and spreading secrets that they trusted you with back in the day. Acting like that only displays how much the breakup affected you and how weak you are.

Don't even think about wasting your energy trying to manipulate others to gang up and destroy your ex just because you despise them. There is no need to turn into the type of person who is constantly busy ruining other people's lives and reputation. Instead, use this time to build your character. Just quietly mind your own business and deal with things like a pro. Before you do something cunning to target the other person, remind yourself that this isn't the best of you, so there is no point in displaying that. Remember that the longer you hold onto your anger against your ex, the more toxic you will become.

If the relationship involved cheating, just be thankful to be set free. Never look back, and never rethink the decision of taking separate paths. Whatever has happened, happened, and it shall stay the same and remain in the past. If you were the one being cheated on, don't be angry, because at least you know that you have done your best when they only did their worst in the relationship. You being cheated on has got nothing to do with you. It was their decision. After all, your ex is the one who will be consumed with envy and guilt when you are off living happily without them. Not just that, but they'll also be busy reaping the karma of their unfaithfulness.

They might apologize or ask you to meet up, or even to take them back, but if they're a cheater, promise me you won't be the one apologizing and asking to meet up or start over. If *they* apologize, fine. Forgive, and move on. Done. It's literally as simple as leaving it at that instead of constantly giving yourself an excuse to revisit the past.

If they ask you to take them back, don't be a fool. You think you miss them? Do you really? What you miss is the memories and the feelings you held toward that person, which can tempt you to run back into the arms that couldn't make you feel safe. Missing someone is a battle between what your mind knows is true and what your heart feels. Don't let your feelings consume you.

A lot of daft people fancy getting back together with the cheater until they have done it about ten times. You should be wiser than that. After all, "Going through old ways won't open new doors," as the saying goes. Bringing them back into your life won't make things where you left off any better, and it won't reverse what happened.

In the end, the relationship is over. Life will go on, without them in your life. And of course, there shouldn't be anyone powerful enough to prevent you from living, especially not them. Don't let your emotions get in the way and convince you otherwise. You need to wake up and stop fantasizing over something, crying yourself to sleep, overthinking the negative thoughts, and repeating the scenes of what happened over again in your head.

You are hurting and it's normal, but please don't make it a habit. That will only make you even more miserable than before. Being depressed and draining your life away until you have no tears left to cry won't help you budge an inch on the road of life. Yes, it's an odd period of time, and what you are going through is tough, but you must make sure you go up from here. Let the experience make you wiser, so you never make the same poor choices and have to go through this same misery again.

Prioritizing Your Personal Growth

Speaking about growth, everyone heals in different ways and at different paces, depending on the person. Your healing is only up to you. No one can force your healing apart from yourself. Only you can help yourself and make yourself rise above your problems, even when you feel you don't have the energy to do it. And even if people constantly drill the words "Move on!" into your head, remember that's only part of what you need to do. Don't *forget* and move on. Instead, move on, but also *remember* and *learn*.

Learn to put your healing and your happiness first. Take this time to grow and explore the world independently— most importantly, for yourself, without anyone else stopping you. You are at an advantage. You have the chance to discover new things that you never knew about yourself when you were in the relationship.

But when I say this, I'm not suggesting you use your sadness and vulnerability as a ticket to carelessly get with other people as a distraction. If you disrupt your healing process, you are just delaying it, and you won't be completely healed by the time you are in another relationship. That only leads to you wasting your time in the future, as the next relationship probably won't work out if you are not healed from within.

Think for a moment about people you know who've broken up. Think about how differently people handle heartbreak. Some become damaged and depressed, sometimes resorting to drugs, smoking, or desperately seeking a new lover to alleviate the pain and the sadness. Since that behavior only provides temporary relief, they just keep repeating them over and over. They do all of these things to distract themselves, making it much harder for them to accept reality later on, just because they refused to adjust to it earlier when the situation was still raw.

Then there are the wise, much brighter individuals, who when their hearts get broken, allow themselves to hurt for a while, accept the way things are, then get back up on their feet and continue thriving. Such persons are the first to heal, the first ones to find happiness. Why? Because they dealt with the heartbreak straightaway. They took in the pain and learned from it the right way. They dropped out of the social whirl and took time to self-reflect and ask themselves: "What can I do to heal myself and improve myself?" This, instead of wondering: "Why does this happen to me?" or "What have I done to deserve this?" It's the difference between the mindset of a positive-thinking person and a negative-thinking person. The positive person knows that no one else can help them but themselves.

Like that person, we should never let heartbreak sting us to the point of doubting things like our self-worth or our ability to love. Those things are a constant. Remember that not many people have a heart like yours. Just this one person shouldn't control or change your views on love. Don't give them that kind of power over you.

Well, this wraps up the whole of the relationship topic. It can get crazy sometimes, but it truly isn't that complicated. In a nutshell, all you need to remember is to *prioritize*.

Chapter Five: Tyrant Technology

> *"I fear the day that technology will surpass our human interaction.*
>
> *The world will have a generation of idiots."*
>
> ~ Albert Einstein

I totally agree with Einstein, since it's literally happening right now in our world. Modern technology is *contagious*, and its power is so strong that it can change an individual on a large scale. So the first half of this chapter is directed to those who can't handle this change beneficially—those who find themselves unable to let go of their gadgets, or the so-called "video game addicts." Then, I will talk about the social media addicts. If you don't play video games, I still recommend that you listen in.

'It's Addicting!'

"It's addicting!" is a phrase we all are familiar with, but how can you tell if you are addicted to video games? Time for you to check a few boxes with a pencil in hand and honesty in mind.

	≤ 1 hour	2 hours	3 hours	4 hours	≥ 5 hours
Roughly how many hours do you spend playing video games every day?					
How often do you think about video games throughout your day?	Never	Barely	Sometimes	Often	Always
How important are video games in your life?	Not at all	Hardly	A bit	Quite	Very
Would you consider your life to be incomplete without video games?	Not at all	Hardly	A bit	Quite	Very

These quick-fire questions are for you to become more aware of how time-consuming video games may be in your life. If the answers you checked are more toward the right side of the page, then you are most likely addicted. Even if you say that spending three hours a day on games isn't much, even if you think about games only a few times a day, even if you think games are only a bit important in your life, and even if you think your life would be only a bit incomplete without video games, you still could be an addict. People tend to not notice how addicted they are, which causes them to check the wrong boxes just because they can't see it. So yes, even if you are extremely addicted, you might say otherwise.

Think about your life before you started playing. Did you start because you wanted time to speed by? To distract yourself from your busy life? Did it give you less stress or did it give you a ton more? Think about how video games have affected you. Reaching the next level might be your only focus, but think about it. Is this the only thing you are willing to live for?

I asked this question to a friend of mine who was jealous that his friend was able to multitask playing video games and getting good grades at the same time. It didn't seem fair to him at all, and he had no explanation for his friend's "superpower." But I told him to think about the scales. Both sides need to balance. It's better to multitask doing two or more beneficial things that will impact your life positively. If you put one bad thing (games) and one good thing (grades) on each side of a scale, of course the bad will outweigh the good, since lack of self-control makes it easy to overdo the bad side. There's a high risk of games and grades clashing, and often it doesn't end well.

Now go back and look at the boxes you checked. This time, have a calculator in hand and multiply the first checked question by seven. The number on your calculator that comes up is roughly the hours you spend a week. Multiply *that* number by fifty-two, and you will get the total hours you've spent on video games in the course of a year.

Blinded from Opportunities

In the past year, if you had spent less time with your games, you could have…

1. Gone out more with family
2. Hung out with friends a lot more
3. Worked out a bit
4. Studied, caught up with schoolwork, or done homework
5. Practiced a musical instrument that is sitting there, collecting dust
6. Developed a new or better habit
7. Achieved a completely different and beneficial goal

All the seven things listed above are various options that you could have gone with when using your time wisely. Circle the ones you believe you can accomplish, and work on them. Write them down on a small post-it note and stick it somewhere in your room. This way, it will be a constant reminder to get yourself out into the world.

Task of the day: take some time off and start small. Take thirty minutes off of the time you would normally spend playing. Then another fifteen minutes the next time, and every day (or every second or third day). Reduce the time you video game by fifteen more minutes. Or you could say to yourself: "I will play for an hour and stop once the clock reaches 6 p.m. When it does, I will find other things to entertain myself with." But of course, these must be things that aren't related to technology.

Regularly limit the hours you spend a day until you develop a habit of being able to control yourself more and more, until you eventually quit, or spend no more than half an hour a day playing video games. The more you do this, the more you will get a grip on life. And when you do, you will wish you could have lived the previous years in a much more sensible way. The more you focus and commit to video games, the less you will focus and commit to real life. Your focus on video games stops you from getting things done, and wrecks your sense of priorities. It prevents you from being present, which stunts your personal growth. You no longer live in the real world, only in a virtual one.

Studies show that excessive gaming causes your brain to release endorphins, which are important for learning and concentration. But it's also the same chemical released when people do drugs. This is why excessive gaming makes people develop gaming disorders, like addiction, which negatively affect the way the brain operates. Shooter games (everyone's well-known favorite) weakens the brain, increasing the risk of dementia later on in life. It also damages the hippocampus, which is a region in the brain that controls and regulates motivation, emotion, learning, and memory. So yes, it's bad.

Along with this, video games are also the culprits responsible for a screwed-up sleep routine, which only worsens your energy levels, mental performance, and emotional well-being. If you are willing to sacrifice all of that for a stupid game, then I hope you know what's in it for you. And I am pretty sure it isn't a new level or a new avatar.

Remember that video games also trigger people's temper and emotions. I am 100% certain that someone (possibly your parents) has more than once scolded you to, "Fix your attitude!" But you just sit there, because you don't even realize how much of an anger issue you are gradually starting to have. All this does is shut you out from the world even more.

I was introduced to games at the age of nine, so trust me, I know what I'm talking about. Most people start at that age, or unfortunately, even younger. It's not surprising, only disappointing. Thankfully, I stopped completely before it got too late. But even though that was the best part of it all, the worst thing was that even though I didn't play for long, it was one of my biggest regrets, ever. And I don't regret things that easily. Most of you have played a whole lot more times than I have, but if I say it's one of my greatest regrets, I can only imagine the regret you will feel when you finally give up the habit—and the relief you will feel when you finally start living.

When I gave up gaming for good, I finally realized the opportunities I passed up while being distracted by something pointless. You've been stuck in your own space and time playing, but everything outside your bubble has been constantly shifting, and people around you are getting the move on and achieving wonderful things. Once your bubble pops, you'll wake up to realize that you have been sleepwalking for several years.

New open doors open up to you every day, but are you willing to walk through? The more you play, the more you become walled off from life and miss out on what it has to offer. "Opportunity never knocks twice," is what my mom says. For example, you might choose to play games at home rather than going out with friends. But what if you were supposed to meet your future partner on that day?

You are more than just a dead zombie, who only comes to life when a gadget is switched on. There is so much more to live for and you hold so much potential. Especially at your young age, you should be building a reputation for yourself away from technology. The hype over technology is only temporary. Three years from now, all the devices we have today will be considered "old-fashioned."

You should use more of your energy to invest in more permanent things, like building relationships and thriving in school. Don't resort to games to escape reality and numb the pain in you. Face it. So, if you have been procrastinating a lot, go back to getting things done. Pick yourself up and do yourself and your family proud.

Before we finish this topic, here are some flabbergasting stories of the day. In 2005, a man visited an internet café in South Korea and played a game called "StarCraft" continuously for *fifty hours* (yes, you read that right). He went into cardiac arrest and died at a local hospital just a few moments after. A seventeen-year-old boy died after reportedly playing video games online for twenty-two days straight. He was rushed to the hospital but was declared dead on arrival. Yet another seventeen-year-old boy spent hours on a PC at home in northern Thailand. His father found him dead, next to a pile of takeaway boxes on his desk. Ever since, his father has been warning other parents not to let their children become addicted to games like his son was.

Gulp. I don't know what to feel about this. Even though you might say "Nah, that won't be me," just keep in mind that it can literally happen to anyone. The next victim is randomly chosen. I really hope this sticks in your mind the next time you open your gadgets to play.

The Disappointment of Our Generation

Let's think for a moment about the great role models from previous generations. They really were something, weren't they? Many of them made remarkable inventions, or did astonishing things that changed the world. Their very names have become household words. With their great actions, those people made history.

If you take a look at how things have changed over the years, you'll be able to spot the differences between how people created legacies back in the day, and how people become "influencers" now. Nowadays, people become hugely famous for lip-syncing videos, while people from older generations worked much harder and only became famous after a decade's worth (or more) of work that changed the world. The "influencers" of our generation aren't influencers at all—they're just bad examples. The influencers and inventors of yesteryear made the effort to do impactful things that actually changed the world. All I can say is, we must seem pathetic to the influencers of the past.

Unlike most of our generation, yesteryear's influencers spent their free time reflecting on how they could make the world a better place, and even more fundamentally, on how they could improve themselves as people. They focused, when they were our age, on discovering their abilities and their potential, on learning new things, and on finding out who they were as individuals.

How does that compare with the teenagers of today? It's quite a different story with us, isn't it? Look at the way previous generations managed stress, work, and relationships, and compare that with our scorecard. Our predecessors aced it all, but we, by contrast, run away from minimal challenges that never scared those of previous generations.

Why is that, though? What changed? It's safe to say that technology is what changed us. It has spoiled our generation, but I believe we are still capable of greater things.

I was in a café some months back and overheard a group of older women criticizing today's teens, saying that we should be more useful, and not rely on technology all the time instead of living. If we weren't so lazy and unfocused, we could create a legacy of our own, at this age in particular. We could easily do that if we wanted to. We could improve ourselves if we made the effort, and prove that our generation isn't what others assume.

When one person of the newest generation acts dumb, everyone assumes that the whole of the population is dumb, and that gives us a bad image. Aren't you tired of people assuming that we belong to the generation that will never be able to do anything productive, apart from scrolling past memes all day and being technoholics? People believe that's what Generation Z (born between 1997 and 2012) is all about. If we can take advantage of technology and not have technology take advantage of us, then we can make a change.

I have witnessed children aged one to four watch videos and play games on their parents' phones. There have been occasions when I saw each and every family member whip out their phones at a dining table. Worst part of it is, families like this don't even socialize with each other. It deeply breaks me to witness this. I have seen couples go on dates. Sweet, right? Until the guy gets his phone out and the girl *waits* for him to put it down. When he doesn't, she goes under his influence and does the same. Seriously, man? You asked her to go out on a date and then you just don't talk to her? And she has to *wait* for you? That's just plain disrespectful. No, that's not a couple. That's a couple of acquaintances. I'm sure you all have seen these things yourselves.

The reason why so many people are like this is because people had a sudden exposure to technology. Back in the day, everything was slow and required people's patience. Photographs, for example, were something to be paid for. Once taken, a photo went through a printing process which took days or even weeks. If you didn't like the photo, you would bin it only after seeing it weeks after it was taken.

Another example: letters. My mother once told me that when she was my age, she wrote letters to her parents every day when she was studying abroad in the UK. It took at least one week for the letter to reach my grandparents, meaning that whatever she wrote was something that happened to her one week ago, which means that they would never actually know what was happening to her right now. But if they did, it would be through a phone call, which used to cost a small fortune per minute.

People back in the day were used to being patient in getting what they wanted and on top of that, it cost them. By contrast, today's technology consists of getting what you want in milliseconds—rapid texts sent once you press "send" and photos snapped immediately without you having to pay or wait for weeks to get them in your hands. Don't like it? Delete it. Today, we can use any form of video-call for free, and it only takes a few seconds to happen. And once technology acts slow, we all get cranky.

From being patient, our parents, who are from Generation X (1961-1981) or Generation Y, known as the Millennials (1981-1996) have gradually grown to become impatient due to their sudden exposure and consumption of technology. Everything suddenly was speeding by, which caused them to expect us to speed up as well. They expect their children to learn things immediately the minute they are taught, which makes the world spin even faster each passing day.

Meet Technology, Our Babysitter

Our parents grew up with such a sudden change, but the pivotal point where it all went wrong was when they started seeing technology as an escape route out of many things, such as taking care of their children. Nowadays, if your child is noisy, just give them a phone. If your baby cries, just play a lullaby on YouTube. If you have work to do, just let your child watch TV for hours until you are done.

This shouldn't be the way children are brought up. Parents nowadays dump their kids with gadgets so that they won't bother them, which basically means they don't take care of their children properly. They don't help them explore their childhood. They barely help them with their homework or color their coloring books with them. Technology is their convenient babysitter. This is exactly what makes parents crappy role models these days. If the parent looks up to technology, you can expect the child to rely on it, and grow up relying on it.

The parent will never feel the ups and downs of parenthood, and they will regret it very much later on. They will wish they could have done a whole lot more, that they neglected, just because of their lack of patience and time with their children when they were little. Children tend to adapt to this antisocial behavior until they eventually become distant from their parents. And when they do, parents tend to blame the child for being that way and for always being on the phone. But it's partially the parents' fault because they exposed their children to technology at a very young age, which makes parents unreliable because they cannot seem to properly educate their children.

So many parents today aren't giving their children a proper childhood. It's sad how when we tell a modern-day kid about a certain thing that made our childhood special, there's a high chance they never even heard of it. I mean, why would they? A lot of kids rarely play with toys anymore. They rely on devices to make their childhood memories for them.

Honestly, my childhood rocked because it was made of so many simple things, and they have become iconic. Things like Furbies, colorful gym scooters, parachutes in PE class, making loom-band bracelets, wearing 'Silly Bandz' to school, bringing Barbies and Polly Pockets everywhere you go, believing in paper fortune tellers, wearing plastic princess high heels, and, back then, slapping bracelets were the biggest flex.

Other things that made your childhood special were falling in love with Troy Bolton from *High School Musical*, dancing to "We're All in This Together," watching Hannah Montana after school, and singing along to "The Best of Both Worlds." "The Suite Life of Zack and Cody," "Wizards of Waverly Place," "Camp Rock," and so many other shows made our childhood unique.

Only late '90s and early 2000s kids will understand. Did those nostalgic memories flood back, and did you smile while reading those words? All of those things have unfortunately become "old-fashioned" but will forever live in our hearts.

With this in mind, when your time of being a parent comes, let your kids have the same childhood as yours, or even better. Reintroduce those special things that made your childhood, and don't let the hype die down. Spend time with your children. Color with them in their coloring books. Sit down with them at the kitchen counter table and help them with their homework. Come back home from work and hug them. Help them take a shower. Sing them to sleep. Brush their hair. Change their diapers with grace. After all, these are things that you will only do for a limited amount of time. Once they are seven or eight, they'll be able to do most of them by themselves, knowing that you were always there to guide them at all times. Most importantly, don't introduce them to technology early.

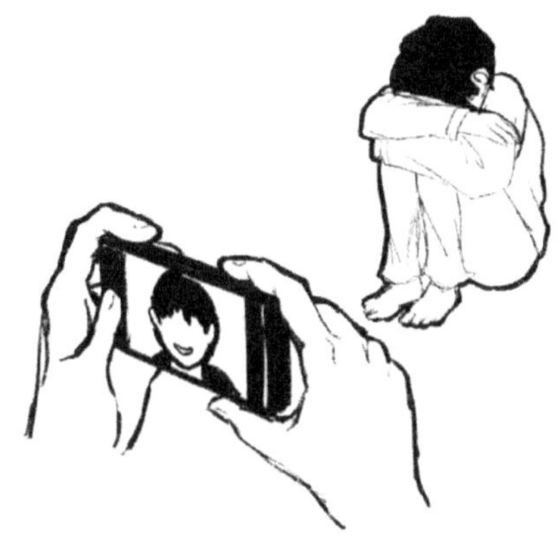

"Social media has created jealous behavior over illusions. Sadly, some people are envious of things, relationships, and lifestyles that don't even exist."

The Wrong Type of Attention

Social media. It's said to be one of the most addicting things in our modern world. Most people won't admit this, but it actually damages our mental health and mindset. It sounds shocking, but it's really not surprising. I already know, and I am pretty sure, if you're honest, that you do, too.

The reason why social media is so addictive is because teens feel the need to constantly chase after likes, flattering comments, and most-viewed stories. We want to become the most-followed out of everyone we know. We grow up living our lives based on numbers and digits. We're basing our lives on an illusion of reality. As someone once observed, "Social media has created jealous behavior over illusions. Sadly, some people are envious of things, relationships, and lifestyles that don't even exist." And this is what makes us a sad generation with happy pictures.

Many teens feel the urge to turn their private lives into something public, so that they can receive greater attention. They are desperate for the appreciation they hope to get online because they can't seem to find it in real life. The validation social media gives them feels great, but what they don't know is, the attention they receive on the internet is the wrong type of attention.

I'm talking about people who feel the need to somehow shine online, whether it's with selfies, beach photos, or pictures of themselves eating at top-quality restaurants with five-star meals. *Snap-snap*, off you go showing it all off, with the objective being to receive virtual envy and adoration. The cycle repeats itself, and the more it does, the more difficult it is to let go. People keep on coming back with more because they *crave* more, but the attention they get in return is superficial and temporary.

Let's get real, after you take a picture and post it online, you only become noticed for a day or two, and then the likes and comments stop, and what you did or posted is forgotten. That makes you feel desperate to come up with something flashy and new to post, so you don't start to feel forgotten and abandoned. It's a vicious circle, and it's pathetic.

Another example of the dangers of social media is online dating and talking to strangers online without knowing who they truly are. Many teens of today love this, which is slightly concerning. I mean, who knows? What if you get catfished? Maybe you will get kidnapped the first time you meet this person. There are so many consequences. Plus, this isn't the real way of dating someone.

Imagine the day you tell your kids that Mom and Dad met on Instagram or Tinder. It's kind of embarrassing, and there is no background story to it. It's just a bunch of horny and desperate people who signed up for a dating app and met there. That's it. *That* is their love story. Instead, you should build your social confidence by meeting people in real life. The love there is genuine, instead of relying on social media to make your social life better.

After all, this is a really clever technique created by those who came up with social media platforms. They already knew what kind of power, consumption, and control it would have over people's lives. They purposely used this secret to win over people's money, and not just that, but their time, too. Time that will never, ever return. And this is why those same inventors are now billionaires.

By contrast, the *right* type of attention comes from real loved ones, like family and friends. This is why the most secure people barely use social media to work on their relationship with their followers. Instead, they would rather work on their relationships with their family and friends in real life, because they know they must invest more of their attention and time in those meaningful things.

Speaking about going online, the reason why we tend to take breaks from the internet is because we all know it's harmful to our own (mental) well-being, yet people still return in a day or two, which isn't a break at all. Think about it. If social media wasn't harmful, then people wouldn't have to take constant breaks, right? If people feel the need to do this, it's a serious problem, and it will only get worse.

And this is what makes social media a toxic and dangerous place. People keep on resorting to it, and they can't stop. The reason why is because people believe they are obliged to display the "perfect" side of their "perfect" life just to prove to others that they are living better lives than they are. And by seeing their posts, you might start to doubt your own lifestyle, and you might start to think that your pictures don't fulfill people's expectations of "perfect."

But the funny thing is, you aren't alone. In fact, they might even be on the exact same page as you. This is why, with each new technology-hooked-generation, people are becoming more depressed, more anxious, more insecure, and more mentally unstable. We lose sight of our self-worth, only seeing ourselves as "not good enough."

So to prove that they *are* "good enough," people film everything, take pictures of everything, and post it, instead of simply enjoying the experience and living in the moment. It's like when people take pictures together, they always say, "Send them to me. I want to post them." Instead of telling their friends to send the pictures over so they can *keep* the memories, they would rather post about it and display it for the public to see. You are more than welcome to post it, but just think about *why* you feel the need to. If you are just doing it for the sole purpose of boasting online, you are an *entertainer*.

Denzel Washington once said, "Just because you don't share it on social media, doesn't mean you're not up to big things. Live it and stay low-key. Privacy is everything." Honestly, he couldn't have said that any better. You don't need the whole world to witness everything you do. Just enjoy the simplicity of life without having the pressure of displaying it to others. This is where you will begin to enjoy and value life at its core, and you'll start to find your self-worth again.

The Art of Photoshop

Be grateful for the wonderful body you were given, instead of photoshopping it into something else. Look at the definition that the social media world brings to the words "hot," "attractive," and "pretty." I mean, it's barely real. People photoshop to get more curves, to appear as if they have rock-hard abs and to make their legs look slimmer and longer. Some even photoshop their faces in selfies to make it appear as if they have no pimples at all. This is what creates and builds up people's expectations of an illusion. Everyone's expectation becomes something completely divorced from reality. And those who can't reach the expectations of other people on social media, get cyberbullied, body-shamed, and fat-shamed for something no one can help about themselves. Behavior like this has become so normalized nowadays, that people think it's something okay to do.

If you do have a beautiful face and body, then good for you. Not many people are blessed to have that. Be grateful you don't need to change a thing while others sit in their photoshop studio for hours. Even if this is the case for you, it doesn't give you an excuse to make others feel inferior or worse about their looks. Don't use it as an excuse to make yourself feel superior. Most of all, don't be the reason for people trying to change themselves.

If you are the one adjusting yourself, there might have been a time when you looked at those models online, thinking, "When can I ever look like them?" But note one thing. The models you see online are probably the most broken of everyone. Their bodies are publicized, objectified, and because of this, they never actually get to cherish them. This causes them to lose their self-worth.

So next time when you look at your flaws, just remember that it's puberty. It's life. It's your face and body. You will never be able to change them, so instead, embrace them. You shouldn't have to change at all to aesthetically please others. Learn how to accept yourself instead of trying to be something you aren't. It's perfectly normal to have acne. It's perfectly teenage to have a flat ass and no curves. Not everyone can wake up the next day looking like an hourglass. Not all guys are born six-feet-tall with rock-hard abs, buff arms, tanned skin, and stunning blue eyes. Some are, but at the same time, some are skinny and lanky, and that's nature. These are the values you need to start loving about yourself, because it makes you, you. You are going to live in this body for the rest of your life. You either come to terms with it, or go against that and suffer.

The more energy you put into "glowing up" and trying to reach some impossible standard of "perfect," the more flawed you actually become. But the more you come to terms with your flaws, the more perfect you become. Maybe not to others but at least to yourself, which is the most important thing. "Perfectly imperfect" is what they say, right? If you learn to embrace the beauty you are given, you will emit and spread that positive energy to those around you until others might even start to vibe with that. And this is where people will begin to notice that beautiful element within you. And once they do, *everything* about you becomes beautiful.

Celebrating Each Other

To finish this chapter off, let's all choose to celebrate, uplift, and empower one another instead of being villains by tearing each other down just because of our looks. After all, it's just appearance. Such mean behavior sparks small and habitual thoughts that run through people's minds and build up until they eventually ruin everything for that individual, especially their self-esteem. Don't be the one who causes people to lack self-acceptance, self-love, self-esteem, and self-respect (all of which are vital) just because you might lack them in life. That's just pure selfishness.

If other people want to shine on social media, let them. Not everyone will shine through appearance. You shouldn't feel pressured to follow in their footsteps. Instead, find a place of your own to shine. Don't look to others to give you the acknowledgment of your worth that you desire. Find that within yourself. Are you posting what you feel comfortable with or are you posting what you want other people to see when they look at you?

People mainly go with the second option. I know so many people (who are insecure but don't think I notice) who post every day about every single thing that occurs in their life, just to make themselves seem busy in other people's eyes. They expose their private life, like recording their bitchy rants and sending them to many others who will be fooled into putting effort into comforting and pampering that person. For me, I have my own problems to solve, and so does everyone. I would rather fix my own first. It's not my job to fix everybody else's. Plus, if they can't help themselves, then how can we?

Please take a few seconds to check the boxes, about your use of social media, in the same way you may have checked the boxes for video games:

How many hours do you spend on social media every day? (Check your screen time on your phone to do this and multiply by 7 to know weekly hours.)	≤ 1 hour	2 hours	3 hours	4 hours	≥ 5 hours
How important is social media in your life?	Not at all	Not much	A bit	Quite	Very
Would you consider your life to be incomplete without social media?	Not at all	Not much	A bit	Quite	Very
Would you be able to go for months without social media?	Can't do that	Probably not	Maybe	Yeah	Definitely

Social media is a drain on our self-love. I implore you to try and take a break for your own good. Delete your most-used app for two weeks to a month as a trial, to see how it feels. Of course, find another way to contact your family and friends, but don't go on any media that contains photos being posted. Once you have deleted the app for a while, realize what a relief it is not to see all those likes and photos floating everywhere. Delete that app to stabilize and prioritize. Delete it to gain self-confidence elsewhere. Delete it for your mental health and well-being. Delete it to feel peace and to live life low-key, but happily. Do it all for yourself.

See it as therapy—something beneficial for you—instead of as something you can't do. The more you think about using the app, the more you will be inclined to get it back. But when you have a thought of going back, distract yourself by doing other, greater things.

For me, that was no problem. Funnily enough, I managed to keep all social media deleted for about half a year while rediscovering myself. What did I gain from that? Even though it may seem like a short while, this helped me immensely with coming to terms with the way I looked because I wasn't bombarded with photos of models with perfect bodies every day. This prevented me from comparing my body to others'. No one should be in competition against other people for the "the ideal body trophy," since there is no such prize. Me being me, and knowing that, I have never felt better.

Go to a mirror, look at your body, and give yourself compliments—whether on the way you look or on your personality and character. Anything works. Really look at yourself and realize how beautiful and blessed you truly are to have come this far, living in your beautiful body, whatever the height, weight, shape, and color. The more you say these beautiful things to yourself, the more you will believe in those positive messages. The more you will love and respect yourself, the more happiness you'll find. After all, don't you deserve that?

Chapter Six: Full Steam Ahead

"Shoot for the moon. Even if you miss, you'll land among the stars."

~ Les Brown

Would your eight-year-old self be proud of who you are today? Take a minute to seriously reflect on the type of person you have become. Let's talk about who you are compared with who you were in the past and where you are headed in the future.

Your Road to Success

There are many things you dream of having, but you might not know exactly where you want to be ten or fifteen years from now. What may be causing this is that you might not have your mind set on specific goals. This could also be the reason why most teens nowadays just go with the flow with everyone else. This is why most of them don't achieve much that's productive and beneficial, and this may be why so many teenagers don't feel worthy.

Having specific goals is the solution to this. Once you're clear on exactly where you're headed, you can start to move in that direction. It's like getting into a car and thinking you are going to end up in some amazing place, without having any idea of where you want to go. You can drive around forever and end up nowhere, because you don't have a goal, a plan, and a direction.

So how do you know what your goals should be? Well, some of them are goals that all of us should have, such as getting into a good school or a good trade program, getting a good job, marrying a good partner, raising a good family, and so on. Other goals will be specific to you personally. Perhaps you have great talent as an artist or wonderful skill with your hands. Pay attention to your talents, and let them guide your future. Also pay attention to intuitions and strong feelings you have about what interests you, as these instincts can be messages from your subconscious about what you are meant to do later on in life.

When you get a signal about what you want to do, you must pursue it. It's something that should never be ignored. Reach out to your nearest resource, and see what develops. Research information about the job or career area you feel motivated to pursue. Talk to some people engaged in that particular trade or profession. See if you can visit their job site, or volunteer to help out at their office. Exposure like that will help you decide if this really is the right trade or profession for you.

These are all the options available to you when physically getting your career up and running. But today, I would like to solely focus on the emotional aspects when it comes to goal setting.

A dream is different from a goal, because a dream is just a wish. It's vague and unfocused. A goal is what a dream becomes when you give it legs, when you turn it into something definite and concrete.

The journey to fulfilling your dreams is undoubtedly going to get rough at times, but that effort is what makes it worth it. Don't fear that side of the journey. It shouldn't turn you off. Instead, it should motivate you. Would your dreams be worth achieving if they required no effort? Waiting and letting what you desire come to you isn't an option, since it will never come unless you put some energy into it.

As Maya Angelou said, "Nothing will work unless you do." Don't just sit there and dream. You can't just depend on circumstances to align perfectly in your life. You can only depend on yourself to actually make things shift and move. Use all you have, and put it forward. Take a look at anyone you admire who has achieved success. Look how far they have come as a person and how much they had to work for it. You are going to have to do the same, or even more, to have and to be what you want in life.

But remember: *give yourself time*. The flower will not blossom on the first day you water the plant, and the fruit will not grow on the day you plant the seed. The longer it takes to grow, the better the result, so let the growth take its time to process.

Don't start thinking you are useless just because you don't know what you want to do in the future. There is plenty of time to find out more things about yourself and what your passion is. Don't rush things. Self-discovery takes months or even years, depending on how much an individual needs to grow and learn. It may be quick to achieve, or it may take a long while to get there. You may face challenges and have lots of learning to do in preparation. You may have zero success today, but gain it all tomorrow. It often depends on the level of your persistence.

The Quotients

This is where the quotients come into play. Not the mathematical ones—I mean your EQ and your IQ. EQ stands for "emotional quotient." It's your attitude and the way you deal with things emotionally. IQ means "intelligence quotient." It has to do with how mentally clever you are.

Let me ask you a question. If you could have only one or the other, would you rather have a high EQ or a high IQ? You might be thinking, "Well, I would love to have a high IQ, because being a bright human being with intellectual abilities is the best thing ever. I mean, who wants to be dumb?"

Personally, I believe that having a high EQ is much more vital. You might debate and argue with me right now, but listen. You could be the cleverest intellect and have the highest IQ ever known, but if you don't have a high EQ or the right attitude to overcome obstacles, then all of your IQ goes to waste. Of course, if you have both high EQ and IQ, then congrats. That's even better. But where a high EQ is required for success in life, a high IQ is not.

Think about it. Some people are highly intelligent, but once the smallest thing gets in the way, they drop everything and run. But if you have a high EQ, you have the open attitude of a learner. You will eventually learn so many new ways of improving, until you will be able to outthink the thinker and outsmart the smarter. You will have learned more than they ever have, and you will have a range in the way you overcome things. And this is what makes you much ahead of the game.

This is why if you aren't motivated to achieve something great, then you won't achieve much, whether you're clever or not. A flexible and resilient attitude is everything.

Maybe right now you feel hopeless, or scared. You may fear that your journey will be never-ending, but know this: everything you're experiencing is changing you for the better. Everything happens to you for a purpose, whether you believe it or not. Trust the process, put one foot in front of the other, and do what you need to do today to move toward the future you'd like to have for yourself tomorrow.

Take this time to be grateful for everything you encounter in life. Count your blessings, because you will never realize how great the journey is until you count the little things. Accept what life has thrown at you. Accepting and learning from these experiences will transform you into a stronger person, bit by bit, every day.

At the same time, don't compare your progress with that of others. They have different challenges to face. The only person you must compare yourself with is your past self. Take your one-year-ago self as an example. If you compare that person with the person you are today, they should be two, almost completely different people.

Even though one year ago doesn't seem like ages ago, look at how much you have changed since then. That's the thing. People grow a lot in one year. We all evolve every day, and this is what makes life so fruitful. This is why you mustn't let your past and future selves down. Your thought of success was in the past, and it's your job to carry it on into the future. What you do today determines where your future self will be. Do a favor for both your past and future selves, and help them end up where they both want to be.

The Meaning of Fear

The only things that will cost you are your patience, your time, and your vow to keep striving. It's not much of a list. If you aren't willing to sacrifice that little bit, then don't expect great things to come your way.

But if you are willing, every day is a day when new doors may open for you. Take the chance to proudly walk through, because you never know what good things may lie on the other side of that door. As the saying goes, "Opportunity never knocks twice." When life offers you an opportunity, you need to engage it, or it will pass on to someone else. When opportunity knocks, will you open the door? As another famous saying goes, "Fortune favors the bold."

Life is kind of like an amusement park. People pay to go on rides that go crazy because that is what makes them a fun ride. If the roller coaster were constantly at the same level and pace, it would be extremely boring. If you were always at the top or always at the bottom, how and when will you actually experience the joy of new things? Fun rides are considered to be those that go up and down because you don't know what to expect next. Up or down, it's life. And life is all about growth, not comfort.

If life goes down at any point, remember that you are the only person who can get yourself out of the hardships you're undergoing. Will you let these situations defeat you without the will to stand up and conquer? If you do, this is the only way you will be defeated. Under no circumstances should anything cause you to miss the opportunity to strive. You get to go through these tough times as you. If you can't help yourself, no one can. Only you can defeat your giant. It's up to you. But remember that those who have made it to the top didn't get there without experiencing their share of scars and bruises.

If you have recently given up on something you wanted because you were afraid, consider that "**F.E.A.R.**" offers a person two options: "**F**orget **E**verything **A**nd **R**un" or "**F**ace **E**verything **A**nd **R**ise." The choice is yours. There will always be challenges wherever we go and whatever stage we are at in life. Each challenge offers a lesson, and learning it makes us wiser. We all have to go through certain lessons, so we might as well accept the fact that challenges will be constantly thrown at us. We need to accept life's challenges and not see them as a disadvantage. Even if horrible things have happened to us, rising above them has made us who we are.

Make friends with your challenges. Study them, and you will start to see a pattern of what you should expect next. Keep those various experiences in mind as you move from one day to the next, because if you don't learn or actually acknowledge an experience, it will keep on happening to you until you eventually do. Indulge the process. See this as an opportunity. To get to the best times, one must go through the worst times. The more we get set back by the worst times, the harder we should try to get to the best ones. Have that extra drive to reach the finish line. From then onwards, all you will do is excel.

There is no reason why you should give it up and let it go if something was *that* important to you. People tend to give up during the pain they are in. Then their opportunity disappears, and there is a high chance that they may never reach their goal, which they had almost attained just before they gave up.

The reason why you strive for something is because you believed it was possible in the first place, so you shouldn't let the obstacles that naturally arise make you think otherwise. Of course you will make mistakes—lots of them—on the way to fulfilling your dreams, but there is no such thing as failure unless you decide to give up.

I love that quote I started the chapter with, so let me remind you of it again: "Shoot for the moon. Even if you miss, you'll land among the stars." Remember why you first aimed and targeted. Even if you don't achieve what you initially wanted to, maybe you will end up somewhere just as great, or maybe even better than you planned. Have a flexible mindset. It's all going to be worth it in the end. The ups and downs of the journey make a fantastic story to tell. And when you share your story with the world, you'll tell them you've lived fruitfully.

Tell them that when you get knocked down to the ground and no one thinks you have what it takes to ever rise again. If you don't feel you've got the strength to get back up and fight, remember these great words of Rupi Kaur: "If you were born with the weakness to fall, you were born with the strength to rise." We will fall and fall again, yet still have sufficient strength to rise back up each time. That's the beauty of life.

There might come a time where you will rise and stay that way forever, but only you can make that possible for yourself. You will look back one day and thank your past self for continuing to strive, for not giving up on you, for making it this far, and for getting you to where you are today, this strong.

If your path to success were simple and easy, you could lose your achievement as easily as you gained it. You wouldn't really cherish what you had attained, and you could easily let it slip away. But if your journey to success is seriously hard to achieve, then what comes after is something great that you will never let go of. It will be yours to keep.

Acknowledging How Far You Have Come

Look at yourself and acknowledge how well you are doing. Stand proud. If no one holds pride for you, I am here to tell you that I do. Appreciate that instead of focusing on what you aren't and what others expect of you. Your dreams could be completely different from those of your parents, your family, your friends, or anyone else. They all will have different views, and some might even pressure you to stop going for your dreams.

Some will be jealous of your determination to succeed, and intentionally try to bring you down. They will say discouraging things to make you feel small, incapable, and unworthy, in hopes that you'll give up. Sometimes even people who up until now have seemed like faithful friends, do this about-face when it appears that we are actually about to succeed. Our potential success threatens them, because it makes them feel small and inferior. Beware of advice and criticism from people who have a jealous streak. They can be the rot at the root of your dreams.

Promise yourself that you won't let such judgments define who you are, or make you decide your goal is impossible and that you aren't worthy of achieving what you've set your heart on. No one else can stop you, but self-doubt can kill all. Negative thoughts can keep on chirping in the background, convincing you to stop, unless you recognize that mindchatter and root it out. Replace such thoughts, when you have them, with a restatement of your goal, your ability, and your determination. Blast out the bad thoughts with good ones. Don't let self-doubt get the better of you.

Thomas Edison invented the lightbulb, the phonograph, film, the motion picture camera, and much more besides. That same man left school to work on a railroad when he was younger. People doubted him, but he grew up to become one of the world's greatest influencers in history.

There is a great story about Edison. He tried again and again to invent the lightbulb, but no luck came. At that point, someone asked him how it felt to have failed so many times. Edison replied, "I haven't failed. I've just found ten thousand ways that a lightbulb won't work."

Damn. I mean, many of you (myself included) would have given up after the *first* try at doing something everyone said was impossible. But in Edison's case, he attempted to do something literally impossible yet so incredible, and in the end, he managed to change the world completely.

If he just gave up after one shot, or after 9,999 shots, imagine how different the world would be today. Light during the day, consuming blackness every night. Candle wax everywhere. One man can change the whole world, and you can, too. Even if you don't aim to do something that earth-shattering, you can change the world you live in for yourself.

Even when others don't acknowledge you, as long as you are happy with the direction you're going, you have already achieved something. You have the satisfaction of working toward your dream. No one can take that from you.

When striving for something, never forget to honor your other priorities as well. Don't exhaust and overextend yourself just to reach that goal. Bit by bit, every day, will suffice. I know many people who are overambitious to the point where they sideline everything, including their health, family, friendships, and relationship. It's said that if your whole life is about achieving something, it won't satisfy you once you achieve it. You must have a balance. Don't be overambitious to the point where you become too attached to work.

I would like to end this book by sharing one last thing. It's something my mother always reminded me of in dark times when I refused to rise above my problems and strive for what I desired in life. She would say, "Happy or sad, the day goes by. Today never comes back, so why not spend it happily?" Finally, I changed my mindset and told myself, "I want to live and spread positive energy. I am going to rock my existence as a teen." This is exactly how I now choose to spend my days.

What my mom said made me realize that living isn't existing. It's a choice. Life isn't just something that is handed to us. It demands that we give it everything we've got.

That brings me to my final question of this book. "How are you going to spend *your* life?" You do know YOLO and YODO—which is short for 'You Only Live Once' and 'You Only Die Once.' You've only got ONE shot at life. The CAPS effect is to remind you of how big of a life you are destined to live. It's a big world out there, and you are just one person. Yet I'm certain you are capable of doing things that are absolutely stunning. Who knows? You might even change the world.

Think wisely. As I've said before, time is ticking…

Chapter Seven: The Biggest Lesson of 2020

As we all entered this year with the fresh mindset of "It's a new decade!" and "The year 2020 is going to be my year to shine!" we all started off with huge ambitions and we set ourselves amazing targets. This year was supposed to be that year where everyone grew, where people started to take things seriously and get their lives together. But it all ended abruptly before it even started when COVID-19 broke out, out of nowhere. I mean, who would've expected that? Just when we decided to make a change in our lives, it was rudely interrupted by something so hideous.

There have been numerous pandemics in the past, but this one is something that all of us have never experienced as a generation. Months went by and more cases and fatalities arose. The world completely stopped and shut down, and people of all nations were on the run. News kept flooding in nonstop, and nobody could catch a breath. No one could ever tell whether or not they or their family members would be the next victims.

All of this contributed to the huge build-up of constant fear and anxiety. Everything escalated and everyone's lives were deeply affected on so many levels. The trauma and paranoia we adopted caused us to hold real fear in our eyes. And above all, people battled over various essential needs, and everyone's main objective switched from *living* to *surviving*.

All of the tragedies and pain took away so many lives of youths who held so much talent and potential. There were people who were destined to live a life full of abundance and adventure. They were supposed to lead a legacy and make a great mark on the world, but they were kept from living that life. We were all stripped of our freedom; the ability to see our relatives; to hug our friends and to kiss our loved ones. Even traveling the world and discovering its beauty was restricted. That was the last straw—the last single shred of happiness.

All of this shook the world, which made us realize how things can easily be stripped away from anyone regardless of their age, wealth, success, or health condition. None of that matters, no matter who we are. And this is exactly what the pandemic proved. We all have taken our normal life for granted, only to realize how much we miss that normal life.

Maybe we have been selfish. Maybe our values have gotten skewed. Maybe we deserved this year's humbling experiences to gain our true values. Maybe the world slowed down so that we could have the chance to catch up to speed and rediscover who we truly are. Maybe God sent us the pandemic just so we could be sent to our rooms to reflect on ourselves and how we have been making our lives purposeful. So in a way, we owe 2020 a debt of gratitude.

Even though you might not agree with me on this, maybe this year was needed for change and growth.

And to be completely honest, I've never found a better way to spend 2020. I might sound stupid for saying this, but hear me out. 2020 is a blessing in disguise. Has no one ever thought of that? Setting aside the various traumatic events this year, if you open your eyes, you'll see how all of it has helped us grow more than we think. This year is the year of awakening. Think about it. Did people actually get to know the real you before 2020 happened? We had so much time on our hands to reflect on ourselves, and because of this, I believe that this year has shaped us into a hugely improved upgrade from who we were the years prior. The year 2020 revealed our true selves to ourselves.

"How?" you may ask. The population of the world is currently split up into two groups. The first group of people are those who just watched Netflix in bed and played video games all day on their couches for almost a year straight. However, the other half of the world's population have wisely spent their entire year doing productive things, even when limited—such as walking in the park, waking up early for a workout, reading, picking up a new hobby, achieving a goal they have tirelessly worked for, etc. You know who you are and which group you belong to.

I myself know that I have accomplished more in the year 2020 than I have so far in my sixteen years of life, even when it shouldn't have been the case. I started writing blogs, my very own *The RichMindz Podcast* started airing on streaming platforms, and hey, after all, I finished writing this book for you. And of course, I explored the many ways I could improve myself as a person. I just kept myself going, and I can tell you, 2020 has been a heck of a ride for me.

All I can tell you is, even when all hope has been seemingly lost this year, just know that the hope we have doesn't come from our surroundings. It comes from within us. Your actions might have become limited, but it doesn't mean that *you* are. This year was the biggest opportunity you had to get yourself out in the world, even when you might not be physically able to.

So, whatever you have set your mind on at the beginning of this year is a target you can definitely get back to and try to achieve again. At the end of the day, not all is lost. It's never too late to get back on track. I encourage you to do something. And once you do, you will feel this slight ounce of hope—maybe the only ounce of hope you'll ever encounter this year, but this hope is something definitely worth holding on to.

The Wake-Up Call

I would just like to say one final thing. Today, it's time to *wake up*.

Wake up and acknowledge how fortunate you are.

Wake up and never take what you are given for granted.

Wake up and learn from the battles you fight every day.

Wake up and give yourself credit for how far you have come.

Wake up and be grateful for where you stand right now.

Wake up to your family and acknowledge their presence.

Wake up to your parents and do your best to honor them.

Wake up to the gift of siblings and embrace their company.

Wake up and realize that you aren't alone in this world.

Wake up to the real friends who have stepped into your life.

Wake up to the people who are gracefully willing to better it.

Wake up to those who surely proved it without a doubt.

Wake up to that special someone and love them wholly.

Wake up and notice the way people treat you.

Wake up to those who mistreat you and walk away.

Wake up to what you truly deserve.

Wake up to your flaws and accept them.

Wake up to your body and embrace it.

Wake up to your health and treasure your well-being.

Wake up to your habits and make a beneficial change.

Wake up and get into that routine you've always wanted.

Wake up and be thankful that you get to do the things you love.

Wake up and find ways to improve yourself as a person.

Wake up to your potential.

But most importantly,

Wake up to who *you* are.

"For I know the plans I have for you,"
declares the Lord, "plans to prosper you
and not to harm you, plans to give you
hope and a future."

~ Jeremiah 29:11

www.ingramcontent.com/pod-product-compliance
Lightning Source LLC
Chambersburg PA
CBHW051830150726
47998CB00001B/367